Gayle)

To healing, growing,
and living our
purpose!

MT

the power of empathy

The POWER
EMP

A Thirty-Day Path to
Personal Growth and Social Change

of

ATHY

Michael Tennant

Illustrations by **Sabrena Khadija**

CHRONICLE BOOKS
SAN FRANCISCO

Library of Congress Cataloging-in-Publication Data available.

ISBN 978-1-7972-2027-7

Manufactured in China.

Design by Vanessa Dina.
Illustrations by Sabrena Khadija.

"Actually Curious" (www.actuallycurious.com), "Five Phases of Empathy"
(www.curiositylab.io), and "Values Exercise" (www.valuesexercise.com)
are trademarks of Curiosity Lab Holdings LLC.

10 9 8 7 6 5 4 3 2 1

Chronicle books and gifts are available at special quantity discounts
to corporations, professional associations, literacy programs, and other
organizations. For details and discount information, please contact our
premiums department at corporatesales@chroniclebooks.com or at
1-800-759-0190.

Chronicle Books LLC
680 Second Street
San Francisco, California 94107
www.chroniclebooks.com

For Chris, Darren, Caroline. For Naya.

For those who have lost a soulmate.

For those who've brought
a soulmate into this world.

For those who are enjoying
their soulmates in the present.

We all seek safety, freedom,
connection, and happiness.

We also compete against our deepest
desires in subtle ways without ever knowing.

Awaken to the agony of our condition.

Awaken to the bounty and
abundance of the world.

I invite you all, my soulmates, to journey
from empathy to emotional prosperity.

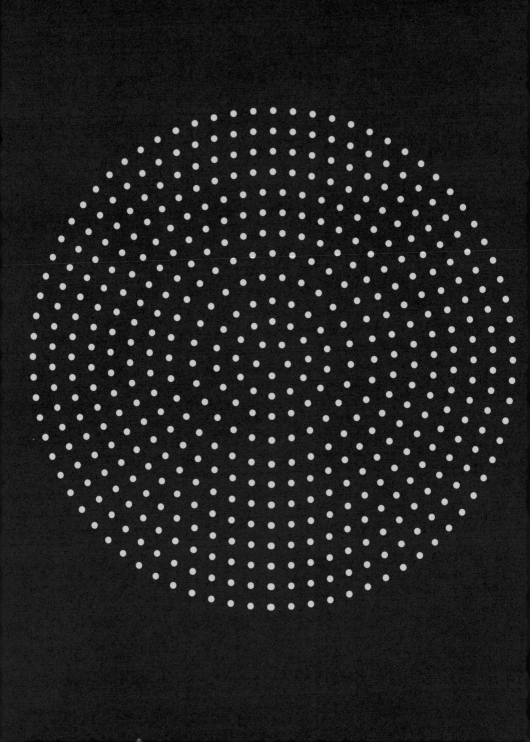

Introduction

The book you hold in your hands is a guide to using the science and psychology of empathy to lead a more fulfilling and purposeful life, while leaving a lasting impact on the world around you. It's also a deeply personal story of healing from grief and addiction, transmuting into a thirst for evolution. The grief I felt, once I was able to be present to listen to it, told me that my life was worth more than how I was living it. Today, that grief has been transformed into the optimistic, altruistic, and idealistic guidebook you hold today. Running parallel to my own struggles with mental health was a global crisis of burnout and mental health issues rising at an alarming rate, as well as ever-increasing instances of exploitation and violence. *The Power of Empathy* is one proposed way of dealing with these issues and for leaving the world a bit better than how we found it.

Not too long ago, the idea of empathy took up a lot less space in my consciousness. In 2017, I had founded a marketing agency called Curiosity Lab, but within two years, the business would be failing and I would suddenly get hit with some deeply felt personal losses. Then the world as we knew it began to experience unprecedented change.

With the arrival of the COVID-19 pandemic, the rise of the racial justice movement following the murder of George Floyd, the US Capitol riot, the rise of anti-Asian violence in America, and the Russian war against Ukraine, it became clear that we needed a tool for navigating the fear and uncertainty around us and for cultivating our individual emotional resilience and well-being.

During this time, I would channel my grief and will to heal and survive into a journey of researching empathy. I began learning tools and routines that would help me learn to let go of grief, past traumas and failures, and the negative mindsets and behaviors that had been holding me back. As a result, anchored in my values and deep awareness of how these events were affecting me, I quickly began to see the connection between my personal healing and the need for healing in the community around me.

8

In 2018, with the approach of midterm elections and the accompanying heated political rhetoric, Curiosity Lab created a card game called Actually Curious to spread empathy and fight divisiveness. The knowledge and tools that we used to create that game and help strangers build trust with one another I now adapted and used for myself. It was this search for self-acceptance and self-compassion that led me to realize how many people are out there just like me, lacking the emotional intelligence necessary to maintain their health and well-being while navigating the uncertain events of our days. Empathy, I realized, was a total market need.

At the time I was writing this book, Mental Health America released their State of Mental Health in America 2021 report[1] indicating that 19 percent or roughly 47 million adults in the United States reported experiencing mental illness, up 2 million from the prior year's report. More alarming are the increasing number of adults with serious thoughts of suicide, which was 4.3 percent in the 2021 report, representing over 10.7 million Americans, and the number of young people ages twelve to seventeen who experienced at least one major depressive episode,

which increased by 13.84 percent to 3.5 million. The report further indicates that close to 10 percent of young people in America cope with severe to major depression, which often coincides with severe anxiety, disorderly behavior, and early substance use.

The rise in instances of depression, anxiety, and other conditions brought on by the world events of 2020 created an unforeseen need for mental health services, which the health care system was not equipped to provide. Major concerns over the lack of mental health providers, especially the shortage among psychiatrists, predates the pandemic. In 2016, the US Department of Health and Human Services (HHS) predicted demand for 250,000 additional mental health workers by 2025.[2] With reported rates of anxiety and depression surging in 2021, from 1 in 10 to 4 in 10 American adults,

9

2. Health Resources and Services Administration/ National Center for Health Workforce Analysis; Substance Abuse and Mental Health Services Administration/Office of Policy, Planning, and Innovation, 2015, National Projections of Supply and Demand for Behavioral Health Practitioners: 2013–2025, 19, https://bhw.hrsa.gov/sites/default /files/bureau-health-workforce/data-research /behavioral-health-2013-2025.pdf.

1. Maddy Reinert, Theresa Nguyen, and Danielle Fritze, "2021 The State of Mental Health in America," 2020, 8, https://mhanational.org/sites/default /files/2021%20State%20of%20Mental%20Health%20 in%20America_0.pdf. Accessed December 28, 2022.

this number is likely now too conservative. The HHS has also designated 6,597 mental health professional shortage areas in the United States—these are geo-graphic areas, population groups, or health care facilities that do not have enough mental health profes-sionals to meet local needs.[3]

With stats like these, an already strained mental health infrastruc-ture was destined to collapse when the pandemic hit. Despite the exhaustive efforts of our mental health workers to expand their hours and caseloads, many vul-nerable people in our communities still do not have adequate access to the critical mental health ser-vices they need. There's no better time than now for individuals to acquire the vital tools needed for empathy and self-care.

* * *

It's not easy to hold space for depression, anxiety, addiction, and suicidal thoughts—even for those you love. I learned this firsthand when my family losses began to pile up between the months of December 2018 and October 2019, beginning with the passing of an uncle in December, an aunt in March, my brother Chris in July, and my brother Darren in October.

Amid the grief I was suffering due to a cascade of family deaths, I also was facing the fallout from the failed relationship with my former romantic and business partner. I had reached an emo-tional rock bottom. By early 2020, I was unemployed for the first time since college, $90,000 in debt, and continuing to battle a decade-plus-long struggle with substance abuse. At thirty-six years old, I needed to move back home and ask my parents for help.

While many of my close friends and family were willing and available to support me for a time, none had the knowledge, training, or even self-awareness to hold space for my pain and appropriately guide me toward support.

The grief I was feeling was exacer-bated by my ongoing struggles with shame and fear of the opinions of friends and family. Prior to all this, I was a very successful media, advertising, and nonprofit execu-tive, and I felt I had a lot to lose if people learned what I was working through. In 2019, in the depth of my depression, I felt isolated, was

11

3. Health Resources & Services Administration, "Health Workforce Shortage Areas," HRSA Data Warehouse, last accessed December 28, 2022, https://data.hrsa.gov/topics/health-workforce /shortage-areas.

lacking in self-confidence, and was desperate for change and connection. I turned to substances for one more night, the weekend my brother Chris died, and felt I was nearing an overdose. If I was going to survive and ever find happiness, I needed to learn to experience my difficult emotions and to find clarity and happiness from within.

When we created the card game Actually Curious in 2018, we had similarly lofty goals in mind. Anchored in our individual and collective values, my former partner and team of four interns set out to achieve a seemingly impossible task—to stem the rising divisiveness in our country. Our intention was to gamify trust building by creating safe spaces for difficult but necessary conversations. By making courageous conversations into a deep listening game, we might bypass the ego and the subconscious to allow for vulnerable sharing, curious listening, and a practice of self-reflection.

But the truth was, up until those tragic losses in 2019, I was incapable of truly doing this work myself. I didn't feel safe within myself, let alone in a group of strangers. I was going to need to learn new coping skills and emotional regulation tools to create the safety to build a trusting relationship with myself as the cornerstone of my survival.

To say that empathy found me when I needed it most is an understatement. Thankfully, before the worst of life's twists occurred, I joined a men's leadership group that was grounded in principles taught by an organization called EVRYMAN, which uses emotional intelligence and vulnerability to teach new skills for self and community connection. As I leaned forward into trusting this group of seven men, I received their nurturing, knowledge, support, and compassionate witnessing, which were cornerstones to my recovery. Coupled with my own exploration through books, podcasts, articles, and daily self-reflection through meditation and journaling, I began to unpack the original five-phase empathy model that underpins this book.

To understand bias, I turned to contemporary authors like Malcolm Gladwell, Dr. Cornel West, Robin DiAngelo, and Dr. Trabian Shorters, as well as classic writers like bell hooks and James Baldwin. To understand fear and vulnerability and how they affect connection and collaboration, I turned to the late Thích Nhất Hạnh, Brené Brown, and Ray Dalio, to name a few. To deepen my understanding of emotional intelligence, I referenced books like Marshall Rosenberg's *Nonviolent Communication*, Daniel Goleman's *Emotional Intelligence*, and Elizabeth Segal's *Social Empathy*. On purpose, clarity, and how the human ego can get in the way, I found guidance on finding my way forward from authors like Simon Sinek, Robert Greene, Mel Robbins, and Michael Singer. Finally, reading works by Peter A. Levine and Bessel van der Kolk's *The Body Keeps the Score* were key to deepening my understanding of somatic experiencing, trauma, and healing. Through this period of research and learning, I grew my confidence in accepting the title of "empathy expert."

My difficult and now invigorating deep engagement within community made it all stick. I leaned deeper into my purpose of sharing tools of empathy, and a community began to form around me. We were united by a shared mission to fight divisiveness and to continue practicing and sharing tools among one another to find healing within ourselves and connection to our individual communities. Together, we channeled this abundance of love and agency into fighting for justice, human rights, and well-being.

Over the past three years, I've been blessed to be invited by hundreds of organizations to learn about my mission to spread empathy. Curiosity Lab has hosted thousands at our live, virtual, and streamed consumer workshops and events. Among our collective community, I've witnessed firsthand the power and potential of empathy in our lives. Empathy is a not-so-secret cheat code for uncovering our true desires and our unique paths to happiness. I've come to view empathy as a kind of "sixth sense" and an essential tool for our survival and engagement with one another. At a time when division is an overwhelmingly dominant, negative force in our world and mental illness continues to rise, empathy is both the antidote and a muscle we can develop to strengthen our connections to ourselves and others. With entrenched beliefs and

13

behaviors of power, scarcity, and aggression, this movement will require a cultural shift in how we treat ourselves and one another to take hold and bring about the social change and emotional prosperity that is possible.

Through my own personal journey through depression and addiction, loss of loved ones, and financial hardship, and then to healing through therapy, community support, independent study, and individual and group practice, I learned that my values and needs weren't clear to me, and thus impacted the clarity of my choices. My lack of clarity also affected how I showed up in groups around me and for myself. I was afraid, upset, and closed off to what might hurt me. Today, I've learned to be open to what feels valuable and energetically aligned, and how to calmly enforce my boundaries where my intuition feels off. These practices have helped me uncover more happiness and abundance than I've ever experienced before. Today, I count among my abundances a loving wife; my first child; more than one million dollars in revenue over the past two years; my first home; healthy parents and nieces and nephews; and a wonderful

network of kind, dynamic, and, of course, *empathetic* friends who are committed to leaving the world safer and healthier than they found it.

The Power of Empathy combines all that I've learned and experienced, through professional and self-directed inquiry, into a comprehensive thirty-day guide that ushers readers on the same journey of self-healing and social impact that I've been on. Whether you are working on becoming a stronger parent or leader, developing tools for individual or professional growth, or simply following your curiosity and ambition to be a better person, this thirty-day journey has something for everyone. It's designed to meet any reader wherever they are in their empathy journey, and to take them a step deeper.

This journey into empathy has led me to meet globally renowned leaders and thought leaders in health, business, education, tech, government, and hospitality. These are individuals who are trying to remain resilient and emotionally grounded for the next surprise and challenge ahead. All sectors and all industries need leaders with empathy and emotional intelligence. I have also met thousands of everyday leaders who, like me, found their calling and voice during the pandemic and realized that by giving their passion and energy to others, they receive far greater returns than when they invest only in themselves. Together we make up a large community of sensitive, strong, kind people who see the connection between self-care and the agency and capacity to make the worlds around them better. I see it as a movement to create *a million empathy experts.*

Recruiting and training a million empathy experts requires two things. First is simply lowering the bar for what it means to be an "empathy expert" so more people see that the skills are attainable and can begin to focus on the benefits to their own lives and the lives of those they care about. If you are self-aware and willing to be a compassionate mediator in your own life and in your community, then congrats, you are in. And second, making it easy to access the education and tools for practicing and strengthening our empathy muscles. By training one million empathy experts, we trust that everyone can improve their empathy skills, and thus collective momentum will begin to take root. The teachers will create and continue a cycle of teaching—our peers, our friends, our loved ones, and most importantly, our kids.

Within these pages, I share the cognitive, emotional, and social science behind empathy, along with interactive exercises to help readers turn empathy into daily practice. Written to be read cover to cover or in small doses (twenty to thirty minutes a day)—if that better suits the reader's rhythm—this book offers discrete, manageable tasks that can be completed at your own pace and returned to time and again for inspiration and advice. I use concepts borrowed from psychology, metaphysics, spirituality, and productivity to help you create your own sustainable empathy rituals. I also weave together real-life stories capturing the years between my founding Curiosity Lab in 2017 through my tragic losses in 2019 and up to the

15

present day as I've healed, wed my best friend, and welcomed my first child. I offer these stories as context to my empathy journey, but more importantly for you to see parts of yourself in my testimony.

I'll take you step-by-step through each of my first five phases of empathy to expand your vision of what empathy is and what it can be in your life. You may notice that throughout the book I refer to the *five* phases, not six, which comprise the essential model I've developed in my teaching and personal practice. The sixth phase, exclusive for this book, is designed for those who wish to take the work into facilitation of groups small and large. It's an expansion of my methodology that prepares you to share what you've learned.

In Phase One, we'll establish a shared understanding of empathy. I'll explore common definitions of empathy and invite readers to explore what their goals and intentions are in picking up this book and to start getting comfortable with themselves and their emotions. This journey is yours to direct as you need and see fit.

In Phase Two, I help readers explore how to translate the self-awareness they cultivated in the first phase into actionable information as they use their emotions as a lens through which to understand their values and intuition. I'll help you see how those values were shaped by the world around you and consider how those values connect to your purpose and mission in life today. Together we'll practice identifying what really matters to you and the abundantly available things that bring you joy and fulfillment.

In Phase Three, we begin to look outward. Armed with the knowledge and practices necessary to understand themselves, readers will begin integrating an awareness of others into their practice of self-empathy as I teach them how to feel progressively more safe, grounded, and present in themselves as they engage with their communities. Key to you taking care of others will be your ability to feel confident when you need space to take care of yourself.

In Phase Four, we'll turn our focus outward and begin to understand how the abilities we cultivated for self-awareness and self-compassion can be used to increase our empathy for others. Our goal in this phase will be to strengthen our ability to quiet our own egos and move past our own biases and circumstances in order to take in the perspective of others. Proactive and radical perspective-taking requires stretching your ability for compassion and strengthening your awareness of your triggers and self-soothing techniques.

In Phase Five, we'll dispel the myths of scarcity and explore the concept of abundance. I'll invite readers to reflect on what they feel they have in excess, and what the world might look like if we moved through our communities embracing an abundance mindset and open to the needs and emotions of others. By identifying and confronting our limiting beliefs about our own abilities, and the possibilities of the world around us, we begin to open new pathways to harmony and abundance.

Finally, in Phase Six, we'll close by exploring how to share our gifts with the world and how we can bring together self-awareness, self-compassion, empathy, and an abundance mindset in order to enact wider change in our societies. Our imagination and capacity toward focused action expands, making our dreams and ambitions possible.

Each phase includes five days, with each day beginning with a reflective question. You are encouraged to answer the question in your mind or on paper and to review your answer after you've completed the day's reading and exercise. These questions help provide before-and-after context on how empathy evolves your thinking on a day-to-day or even exercise-to-exercise basis. The questions are

17

meant to open your imagination and allow you to bring your current knowledge to the forefront. After reading the day's lessons, some of your current knowledge may be affirmed, some expanded, some challenged.

I recommend that you read each day the night before and do the exercise first thing in the morning. This will allow the ideas to sit in your subconscious, giving yourself space to complete the exercise within the full day ahead.

Some of the exercises may produce triggering emotions. The days and exercises were designed to be completed in thirty days, but the pace of this work should be determined by you. I want you to feel safe and secure on a day-to-day basis. I encourage you to practice what you are learning immediately by listening to your body and emotions for signals that indicate the need to take extra space between the days or to seek professional support to unpack a key topic.

Often I like to create an emotional container for myself when I need to explore difficult situations, memories, feelings, sensations, thoughts, and cravings. An emotional container is an imaginary tool that therapists use to make clients feel safe when exploring difficult topics. To create an emotional container, you might hear a mediator say something to the effect of "What's said here, stays here. What's learned here, leaves here." Or in a group setting: "Honor the wisdom of others by giving uninterrupted space to share." And there are other examples. You can use an emotional container for yourself and by yourself or in any interpersonal interaction where you are aware that a trauma or significant disruption exists.

Over the next thirty days, we'll learn not only to sit within and learn from our own emotions, but also to use what we learn to deeply embody the emotions of another. By learning to deeply embody the emotions we encounter, we begin to extract crucial information on how to support others in that moment as well as how to respond to similar situations in the future. Throughout the book, I will reference this responsive state as *attunement*. It will become an essential tool as we practice noticing our own emotions and those of others.

With this book, I'm excited to share all that I've learned and help you dig deep to understand empathy and the joy of making it a lifelong practice. By the time you've completed the book, you'll immediately be able to take the questions "How am I?" and "How are you?" to immensely deeper levels than you have in the past. Your ability to accurately place your own emotions will be enhanced. Your ability to take the perspective of others, in good times and in bad, will be expanded. And your intuition toward what to do in challenging times, or to bring yourself expanded nourishment and happiness, will sharpen. More fulfilled and more resilient, we'll channel our collective capacity as proactive emotional leaders—compassionately supporting, courageously confronting, gracefully

modeling, effectively resolving, masterfully connecting. United in our desire for change, we can bridge the gaps that exist within and between us and be more effective in our battles for human rights and for collective well-being.

This is my hope and my goal: that this book will create an army of empathy experts, spreading tools of self-care and compassion in our lives that help bring our communities to places of abundance. And that we will work together to forever redefine how we live and support one another in all phases of our lives.

19

PHASE ONE
The Language of Feelings

Before we dive in, I invite you to slow down and take a deep breath. Check in with what is present for you using whatever awareness, tools, and words you have at your disposal. We are about to embark on a journey together. And the destination will ultimately be guided by you.

It brings me great joy to surrender the pace and the outcome to you. It reminds me of my own journey, and a simple commonality that makes us human: We all have feelings. And those feelings help guide us to our actions, beliefs, and values. I'm inviting you to explore the process of connecting feelings to actions.

The first phase of empathy, the Language of Feelings, explores common ways that empathy has been defined and how it has been applied in our society. The goal is to give you a solid foundation to build upon as you progress through the thirty days. These early lessons will teach you the basic knowledge you need to achieve results and to protect your well-being. We'll also do exercises that isolate key skills and deepen your awareness and ability to use this fundamental knowledge.

The truth is, you've always had empathy skills, and you've subconsciously used them to stay alive. This is not an exaggeration. Our empathy is rooted in our ability to understand the nuances of feelings. Together, we'll explore how the main function of our feelings is actually a quite primitive adaptation of our natural will to survive.

The functions that we'll explore have been running in the background of your consciousness and interacting with your ego at such a pace that it goes unrecognized. We'll begin to notice that the same pace of reaction required in life-and-death situations gets applied on a day-to-day basis whenever our safety or status in the world feels threatened.

Together, we'll learn to watch these processes in slow motion.

Imagine a time when you've seen a high-performance athlete, animal, or machine slowed down so that you can see the intricacies of their skill. Now imagine that same slow-motion technology applied to your own remarkable being. Your primal instincts, how you react to people and situations, unfolded before your eyes in intricate detail. That self-knowledge is what we will aspire to on our clearest and most attuned days.

As readers, you may be coming to this book with different goals. Some of you might wish to use empathy to communicate strategically and build relationships professionally. Others might be looking to close gaps in understanding and to build trust with people you care about or even those that you disagree with. Many of you will turn to this book to support your own healing and growth and to understand your subconscious needs and desires, strengths and weaknesses, fears and passions. Whatever your goal may be, to truly unlock the power of empathy, it's important to have foundational knowledge and skills that will help you slow down and tap into the wisdom that lies within.

The Language of Feelings phase will strengthen your ability to mindfully listen to yourself and to the people and situations around you. We'll learn about the three types of empathy and how they work together to provide us with additional information about ourselves, our colleagues, and our life's situations. We'll learn how to bring emotional insight into our daily decision-making processes. We will discover that by mining the wisdom within our own experiences—past, present, and imagined—we strengthen a new and powerful muscle that we can use to improve our own lives as well as to make an impact on our communities.

My goal isn't to make you overly sympathetic, agreeable, vulnerable, or any of the outcomes commonly mentioned by individuals who've expressed trepidation about becoming "more empathetic." My goal is to proliferate a shared understanding of what empathy can do for our personal and collective well-being, and to share easy ways to identify shifts in emotions. By bringing greater attentiveness and intention to how we respond to people and situations, we individually affect our collective mental well-being.

I repeat: The work you do on yourself to become more aware and to feel more grounded has a ripple effect that improves our collective well-being. By modeling compassion, we actually unlock a greater capacity for compassion and agency in our daily encounters.

I invite you to surrender your ego to the outcome and see where your feelings guide you over the next thirty days. Now let's dive in.

Empathy as a Tool

Are you ready to unlock the power of empathy?

Even before you picked up this book, you probably heard the word *empathy* mentioned a few thousand times. The word has permeated all parts of our society. As we figure out how to navigate difficult conversations around race, gender, sexuality, climate change, mental health, COVID-19, war, the economy, and so much more, it always seems to come back to empathy. Perhaps the reason we turn to empathy is because we haven't yet lost hope. It's a skill and a value that can bring people together.

If you search for the word *empathy* on Google, the first definition you'll likely find is "the ability to understand and share the feelings of another,"[1] which makes empathy sound more like a superpower than

a learnable skill. *Psychology Today* defines empathy as

the ability to recognize, understand, and share the thoughts and feelings of another person, animal, or fictional character. Developing empathy is crucial for establishing relationships and behaving compassionately. It involves experiencing another person's point of view, rather than just one's own, and enables prosocial or helping behaviors that come from within, rather than being forced.[2]

What stands out most about this definition is its focus on the external—on how empathy helps us form relationships and be useful to *others*. It's no wonder so many have joined in on the journey to unpack all that empathy can be and all that it can enable. Empathy is a superpower we can learn, and use, to strengthen our ability

23

1. "Empathy," *Oxford Learner's Dictionaries*, last accessed October 17, 2022, https://www.oxfordlearnersdictionaries.com/definition/english/empathy.

2. *Psychology Today* staff, "Empathy," *Psychology Today*, last accessed November 14, 2022, https://www.psychologytoday.com/us/basics/empathy.

to engage with the world in a positive way.

A key misconception about empathy is how it relates to sympathy, a similar yet distinctly different experience. Although both terms account for how someone feels, sympathy is more about how you feel than how the other person feels. To feel sympathy for a person or a situation is to try to understand what might be unfolding, and to focus attention on how that situation makes *you* feel. It removes attention from the person or situation at hand and makes it about you. We lose the ability to receive a person or situation fully when our attention shifts to the emotions stirred inside us. Empathy, as you will learn throughout this book, goes much deeper, to consider your and the other person's needs, and therefore has utility for all parties.

Empathy can help us be better family members and romantic partners. Famed relationship researcher and therapist Dr. John Gottman describes empathy as mirroring a partner's feelings in a way that lets them know that their feelings are understood and shared. Empathy can also be the key factor in resolving conflicts. Dr. Marshall Rosenberg, the creator of the nonviolent communication framework and the book by the same name, uses compassion, understanding, and empathy to transform how we approach wars and everyday conflicts. Dr. Daniel Siegel, a clinical professor of psychiatry and executive director of the Mindsight Institute, teaches how an understanding of neurobiology and empathy can help us regulate emotions and respond constructively to stressful and unexpected situations.

Numerous elementary, middle, and high schools across the country have adopted Social and Emotional Learning (SEL) programs for children of all backgrounds, particularly to support those who come from ethnic and low-income and under-resourced populations. These programs are designed to stem the long-term effects of adverse childhood experiences that are statistically proven to lead to difficult adult lives.

But what I have learned in my own journey into empathy is that with the rise in mental health struggles and workplace burnout, both of which I have direct and ongoing experience with, it's just as important to be able to understand, comfort, and prepare ourselves in difficult situations as it is to help others.

For me, this journey began out of dire need—a will to survive that pointed me in the direction of increasing my own self-compassion. My ability to forgive myself was crucial to giving myself permission to release the grudges, toxic habits, behaviors, and ways of thinking that were blocking my ability to love myself and others. In effect, I needed self-empathy.

It was Dr. Marshall Rosenberg who coined the term *self-empathy* and who said, "We need to receive empathy to give empathy."[3] According to Dr. Rosenberg, when we are triggered by something that occurs or that is said or done by another person, we need "to stop, breathe, and give ourselves empathy." Something in us informs our reactions, and when we have self-empathy, we are willing to understand what that something is: the past beliefs and experiences informing our reactions in the present moment.

As I've absorbed this work from Dr. Rosenberg while on my empathy journey, I've come to understand that empathy is a way of life. It's about strengthening the tools we need to bring emotional awareness more prominently into our daily decision-making

---

3. PuddleDancer Press, "Marshall Rosenberg's NVC Quotes," Nonviolent Communication Books & Resources, last accessed November 14, 2022, https://www.nonviolentcommunication.com /resources/mbr-quotes.

and communication with one another. Empathy is active and ongoing, always present and available, and once we cultivate the right skills and activate our awareness and intention, empathy is exponentially increasing.

No matter who you are or why you've picked up this book, your journey into empathy starts with you. Before you can turn your lens outward, you need to trust yourself to be able to deal with the entire spectrum of emotions that may arise in any given circumstance.

Here on Day 1, let's focus on setting intentions for your journey into empathy. In this exercise, let's create the emotional container for you to contemplate your own meaning of empathy and the expectations and desires you're bringing into this exploration. Join me in a journaling exercise that explores what empathy means to you, and unearth the purpose of strengthening your capacity for empathy.

DAY 1

After creating a safe space for intentional self-discovery, take some time to consider and answer the following questions:

What does *empathy* mean to you?

What thoughts or judgments come to mind when you think about empathy?

What is your desired outcome for this exploration of empathy?

The Five Core Emotions

What emotions do you struggle most with expressing?

Our minds and nervous systems can become efficient at avoiding some emotions during particularly challenging or awkward moments. It's like an emergency off switch. The emotion gets too intense and we react outside of our norm without even realizing. Our normal way of being and engaging can change suddenly without us knowing, let alone understanding the reasons why. I didn't learn this about myself until well into my thirties, but this would happen to me in situations where I received unexpected questions from people in positions of authority. As an introverted-leaning person, I had this happen in times when I was excited to speak to a person I had just met. Those split-second reactions to avoid a difficult emotion can end up being the difference between a warm first impression and a cold one, a smart financial decision and a rash one, a trust-building interaction and a damaging one, acting on a gut feeling and letting the moment pass you by.

By familiarizing yourself with the five core emotions, you can expand your ability to notice, accurately identify, and proactively respond to your emotions. Even more, with this level of emotional attunement (meaning how responsive you are to your own or someone else's emotional needs), you'll be better prepared to respond when unexpected, heightened emotions inevitably arrive.

Sadly, many of us live in a cycle of avoiding our emotions. This avoidance might play an important part in helping us feel safe and functional amid difficult realities. To express emotion might not be "your thing," and I get it! When I do empathy workshops in organizations where attendance is mandatory or strongly encouraged, I notice several people who are resistant to any kind of emotional expression. I have empathy and compassion for

28

them; historically, work environments have not been a place where emotions are welcomed. I'd go further to say, from my own experience working in nonprofit and for-profit organizations, that workplaces can be rife with judgment-led and passive-aggressive communication.

It's easier to gossip and be indirect than it is to confront emotionally charged situations directly and constructively. Most of us haven't been trained in crisis or conflict mitigation. And surely, most of us haven't learned to default to compassion and curiosity before anger and hurt.

Emotional expression in the future workplace is important for two reasons. First is the massive amount of time that we spend at work. The majority of Americans spend about eight hours a day physically at a work location.[4] That's roughly 50 percent of our waking hours. Most of us need our jobs to survive. A workplace culture that discourages or is ill-equipped to handle emotional nuance is poorly prepared to confront rapid change, social and economic disruption, and the well-being of the future workforce.

This leads to my second reason. Commonly, unexpressed emotions can boil over into frequent complaints, disagreements, or blowups with the people we care about or are responsible for. Our friends, families, coworkers, and even our own bodies feel the fallout from emotions that aren't constructively explored and expressed. Prolonged, they build into unexpected problems like lapses in communication, inefficiencies, burnout, depression, anxiety, addictions, and even suicide. As I discussed in the intro to this book, instances of burnout and

4. Bureau of Labor Statistics, US Department of Labor, "American Time Use Survey—2021 Results," June 23, 2022, https://www.bls.gov/news.release /pdf/atus.pdf.

issues of mental health have been rising at an alarming rate.

Currently, two-thirds of full-time employees experienced burnout at one time or another,[5] and more than a third of workers claim their employers have no internal solutions for their well-being. Mental Health America, in their 2021 State of Mental Health in America report,[6] notes that 47.1 million Americans (that's almost 1 in 5 individuals) are dealing with some kind of mental health condition. Depression, anxiety, and suicidal ideation are all on the rise.

Research on the long-term effects of emotional suppression and repression highlights the importance of emotional expression on our individual lives and bodies. A 2018

research report for the *International Journal of Psychotherapy Practice and Research* entitled "Consequences of Repression of Emotion: Physical Health, Mental Health and General Well-Being"[7] found that "patients with difficulties in managing their emotions subject their health and well-being into gross negligence and as a result are more likely to display a history of substance abuse, poor nutrition, disordered eating, lack of exercise, abnormal sleep patterns, poor compliance with medical interventions, and behaviors that are injurious to oneself."

The study suggested that individuals who cannot manage difficult emotions tend to be more difficult patients and end up getting in the way of their treatment, stating that it is "the protracted reliance on self-defense against the expression

5. Georgi Todorov, "Important Burnout Stats, Trends and Facts 2022," last updated October 17, 2022, https://thrivemyway.com/burnout-stats.

6. Maddy Reinert, Theresa Nguyen, and Danielle Fritze, "2021, The State of Mental Health in America," 2020, https://mhanational.org /sites/default/files/2021%20State%20of%20 Mental%20Health%20in%20America_0.pdf.

7. Jainish Patel and Prittesh Patel, "Consequences of Repression of Emotion: Physical Health, Mental Health and General Well-Being," *International Journal of Psychotherapy Practice and Research* 1, no. 3 (February 15, 2019): 16–21, https://openaccesspub.org/ijpr/article/999.

of emotions and feelings that creates the tension required for the disease to thrive." Emotional expression and healthy regulation even has an effect on aging and longevity. The study found,

psychological factors bordering on emotions are more important predictors of a long, healthy life than other factors like diet and activeness. Individuals who remain actively involved in issues of life have a sense of hope and sheer optimism and can deal with moments of sadness by finding purpose and meaning, instead of bowing to depressed [sic] and despondency. They are also more likely to live longer and healthier than their pessimistic counterparts. (30)

It wasn't until well after my own emotional rock bottom—and one of my last encounters with turning to toxic substances to numb my emotions—that I realized I so routinely escaped from my emotions that even a gentle inquiry into my ability to feel

(from my partner or my therapist) would trigger a defensive response. And even after I channeled the clarity to realize that I needed to change my toxic coping mechanisms or risk shortening my life, it would take years of patient self-inquiry and individual and group-assisted therapy to truly see how avoidant of emotions I really was (and at times continue to be). It is not easy to share this fact. Even I, an empathy expert, have difficulty feeling all the emotions of my past and present. This awareness brings up fear and shame that I must accept in order to share a truth that keeps me in my integrity and gives you the opportunity to learn from my example.

A prerequisite of empathy is the ability to feel emotions with clarity. How can we truly help another person feel seen and heard if we don't understand the experience of the emotion itself? If the pain someone experiences is similar to an emotion that we ourselves have been avoiding, then it might be challenging to show empathy rather than sympathy.

On my own journey into empathy, one of the earliest revelations that I uncovered was that I had a hard time understanding and experiencing joy. Whenever I experienced a win in my life or in my profession, I'd celebrate for a night with alcohol and drugs, and the next day, return to focus on what was going wrong in my life. My own struggles with joy made it difficult to feel joy for others as they celebrated their own wins and accomplishments.

I was very much seeking to feel joy, and my challenges with it had a negative effect on my love life. Through patient and accepting observation, I learned that I often turned to joyful and extroverted romantic partners who seemed to exude the joy I so wanted to feel. With them, I could easily recognize joy and share in the ways we co-created it for ourselves. However, I'd eventually find myself feeling resentful of how easily they experienced joy. My focus was on their lack of understanding of how my past got in the way of my joy. The lingering emotions that came with that way of focusing were impeding my happiness and would lead me to create distance and conflict.

It wasn't until 2019, when I was living alone while navigating the consecutive deaths of two of my older brothers, that I began to reprogram my mind and body to heal from the traumas of my past. That series of events left me without several of the human anchors to which I tethered my happiness. Fortunately, I found the will to survive within myself. In the summer of 2019, I read *The Book of Joy: Lasting Happiness in a Changing World*, by the 14th Dalai Lama and Desmond Tutu, and began to deeply understand the choice we have in allowing our emotions to direct and influence our lives. The book reads,

Adversity, illness, and death are real and inevitable. We choose whether to add to these unavoidable facts of life with the suffering that we create in our own minds and hearts ... the chosen suffering. The more we make a different choice, to heal our own suffering, the more we can turn to others and help to address their suffering with the laughter-filled, tear-stained eyes of the heart. And the more we turn away from our self-regard to wipe the tears from the eyes of another, the more—incredibly—we are able to hear, to heal, and to transcend our own suffering. This is the true secret to joy.[8]

Scientists commonly group emotions into five core categories—joy, fear, anger, shame, and sadness. For Day 2, I invite you to become familiar with these emotions and to explore them without judgment (there are no bad or good emotions) and with deep curiosity.

Regardless of where you are on your own journey of emotional self-awareness, our collective exploration of empathy starts with a ritual of checking in with ourselves to make note of what emotions we might be feeling throughout our days. This is a practice we will return to over and over until we have established a ritual, so no shortcuts.

8. Dalai Lama and Desmond Tutu, *The Book of Joy: Lasting Happiness in a Changing World* (New York: Avery Publishing, 2016), 322.

DAY 2

Exercise

For today's exercise, we've developed a worksheet called the emotional proficiency audit to help you create an overview of your relationship with the five core emotions. An emotional proficiency audit will come easier to those who have an established mindfulness or yoga practice, as they will already be used to using their breath as a way to ground themselves and create space to scan the body and mind and reflect on what they find.

1. For those of you who are new to this form of self-reflection—your lesson begins now. Take notice of whether feelings of joy, fear, anger, shame, and sadness arise as you complete the chart. This process of noticing, as we've discussed throughout this chapter, is actually a mindfulness practice within itself, so you are already on your way!

2. To set the conditions for curiosity and maximum attunement—find a place where you will be able to relax and have an uninterrupted moment to yourself. You'll need at least twenty minutes.

3. Activate your attunement by placing your feet firmly on the ground, and sit with your back supported and neck aligned before taking three slow deep breaths, each one followed by a long, slow exhale.

4. After you've grounded into your body, begin to access your experiences of deep emotions past and present. Now you're ready to dive into the chart that follows.

Reference the following chart and populate it with an example of a time you experienced each emotion.

JOY	Think of a time in your life when you experienced great joy. When was it? Where were you? Who was there? As you think of the joy you felt, what sensations show up in your body? On a scale of 1 (difficult) to 5 (easy and enjoyable), how was it experiencing joy? Why is that?
FEAR	Think of a time in your life when you experienced fear. When was it? Where were you? Who was there? As you think of the fear you felt, what sensations show up in your body? On a scale of 1 (difficult) to 5 (easy and enjoyable), how was it experiencing fear? Why is that?
ANGER	Think of a time in your life when you experienced anger. When was it? Where were you? Who was there? As you think of the anger you felt, what sensations show up in your body? On a scale of 1 (difficult) to 5 (easy and enjoyable), how was it experiencing anger? Why is that?
SADNESS	Think of a time in your life when you experienced feelings of sadness. When was it? Where were you? Who was there? As you think of the sadness you felt, what sensations show up in your body? On a scale of 1 (difficult) to 5 (easy and enjoyable), how was it experiencing sadness? Why is that?
SHAME	Think of a time in your life when you experienced feelings of shame in yourself. When was it? Where were you? Who was there? As you think of the shame you felt, what sensations show up in your body? On a scale of 1 (difficult) to 5 (easy and enjoyable), how was it experiencing shame? Why is that?

Congratulations, you have just completed Day 2, the Five Core Emotions. Though we are early in our exploration, this was not an easy exercise. We do this exercise to create a map of our own areas of resistance and growth. I invite you to reflect on which emotions you have ease experiencing and which emotions you have difficulty experiencing. Begin the practice of compassionate acceptance, noting all the experiences as parts of you deserving of attention and love. Allow yourself space to replenish and reflect before sharing your discoveries with the world around you. For now, we'll get the most out of this work by focusing our attention inward.

38

What does empathy mean to you?

Like many prevalent concepts, empathy means different things to different people. As we work through this book, take notice of how your definition, understanding, and ease of use of the word *empathy* expands from day to day. Your progress in this way portends what might be possible over a lifetime of increased awareness around empathy. Continue to approach empathy with curiosity, with the intention to reexamine what you already know and to learn what you don't.

For Day 3, the Three Types of Empathy, we will explore the frameworks through which the psychology community and society at large have come to understand empathy. Popularized by psychologists Paul Ekman and Daniel Goleman, the three types of empathy refer to three distinct categories of empathy that work together to help us navigate, motivate, support, and collaborate toward our ambitions and goals.

Dr. Paul Ekman is an American psychologist who is considered a pioneer in the study of emotions and their relation to facial expressions. He is considered the world's deception detection expert, and he sits among the most cited psychologists of the twentieth century for his work discovering and researching micro-expressions. Ekman's work on micro-expressions reveals that our brain is a supercomputer for detecting and reacting to danger—whether that is a primitive form of danger like our evolutionary ancestors would have experienced, such as noticing a saber-tooth tiger stalking prey in the brush, or any modern-day situation that impacts our ego, perception, or status. Just like an animal in the wild, when we feel fear we react instantaneously, choosing fight, flight, freeze, or fawn. When we fear we might be caught in a lie, our bodies react with micro-expressions that are detectable to a viewer skilled at recognizing minute changes. In fact, empathy is a prerequisite for lie detection. When a lie detector test is performed, the test administrator as well as the machine are looking for irregularities in the emotional response of the person they are testing. To identify those emotional irregularities, you must also understand them.

Dr. Daniel Goleman is an American psychologist, journalist, and author best known for his work writing on brain and behavioral psychology for the *New York Times* and for his 1995 bestselling book, *Emotional Intelligence*. In *Emotional Intelligence,* Goleman introduces four key components to emotional intelligence, or EQ: self-awareness, self-management, social awareness (of which empathy is a core element), and relationship management.[9]

9. Crystal Ott, "What is Emotional Intelligence?" Ohio 4-H Youth Development, Ohio State University Extension, https://ohio4h.org/sites /ohio4h/files/imce/Emotional%20Intelligence%20 Background.pdf.

According to Goleman, self-awareness refers to the ability to notice both our individual mood and our thoughts about that mood. By reading and accurately understanding our own emotions, as well as the impact they have on others, we strengthen our ability to manage and control how we respond to others.

Self-management, or self-regulation, is the ability to manage one's actions, thoughts, and feelings in a way that contributes to one's sense of well-being, self-confidence, and chemistry with others. The self-regulating individual is able to take their own emotional responses as cues for their action and self-care, in and out of relationships. Self-awareness is a requirement for self-management.

Social awareness, for Goleman, is where empathy comes into play. It is about using our capacity for empathy to sense what other people may be thinking and feeling, and using it to take their perspective. Goleman explains that this ability comes from neurons in our brain's extended circuitry that connect to the amygdala, the part of the brain responsible for stored memory and for processing and responding quickly to fearful and threatening stimuli. Social awareness translates into our ability to read cues like a person's facial expression, voice, and posture and to adapt how we engage with them. Our brains notice how others respond, and the amygdala and connected circuits translate that information into details about the emotional quality of the situation. This is all instantaneous and most often unconscious. The more aware we are of the emotional tendencies and patterns of individuals and groups, as well as our own, the easier it is to recognize when and how circumstances may be affecting everyone involved. As such, we are generally more attuned to people we are closest to, like family, or people we are familiar with, like those

from a similar ethnic or cultural group or geographic or economic background. This is where unconscious and implicit biases come into play—we might unconsciously prefer or get along with someone more quickly because we are more familiar with their tendencies and behaviors. Social awareness is about noticing the emotional experiences of the people in the room as well as your own emotions and responding in a way that is supportive and constructive.

Finally, relationship management refers to the ability to take one's own emotions, the emotions of others, and the context and produce a successful result. Relationship management is the most outcome-oriented as it mainly deals with using the first three pillars of emotional intelligence to influence those around us. This pillar helps us predict and sense others' reactions and fine-tune our plans and delivery to create a positive outcome. It helps in dealing with situations of anticipated conflict by supporting our ability to see conflicts forming and take steps to address and quell them.

After a series of conversations between Eckman and Goleman around 2008 called "Wired to Connect," Goleman credited Eckman with distilling empathy into three distinct categories that we now refer to as the three types of empathy: cognitive empathy, somatic or emotional empathy, and affective empathy.

Cognitive empathy refers to the ability to understand the five core emotions on an intellectual level. This is the most practiced form of empathy. As we go through our days, we make statements about how we might be feeling or greet others by asking how they are feeling. Cognitive empathy is a common trait among most leaders and people managers. We use this form of empathy to try to understand how others might be thinking or feeling. Sometimes referred to as

perspective-taking, cognitive empathy helps us prepare for negotiations and other situations in which we need to motivate other people.

When I teach about cognitive empathy in my workshops, I like to use the example of a research scientist who has studied behavior in depth but has very little experience engaging with the people they are studying. They may be very knowledgeable and yet stumble across human or commonsense gaps when applying their research. The blind spot to this form of empathy is that we can attempt to understand another's opinion while remaining completely detached from their situation. One way that this might play out is with a person having curiosity about tracking the feelings and thoughts of others, but responding in a way that doesn't consider the emotions and vulnerability of the other person. In extreme cases, as might apply with narcissists, Machiavellians, and sociopaths, cognitive empathy might be used to deceive, manipulate, or even cause premeditated psychological pain. In a less extreme example, I sometimes have to catch myself before I smile, out of pride in my advanced attunement, when I've accurately noticed someone's difficult emotions before they have shared them explicitly with me. If I were to smile, my unintentional reaction might be perceived as mocking, rude, or insensitive.

Somatic empathy (also called emotional empathy), the ability to feel emotions or evoke emotion through language or creative expression, is the balancing element to cognitive empathy. The next time you say the words "I feel your pain," you are referring to this form of empathy. Somatic empathy sits within the field of neuroscience and deals with our brain's ability to recall expressions, memories, and events in a deeply felt sense. As Eckman would attest, this evolutionary knowledge is responsible for a baby's ability to communicate needs through facial expressions, gestures, and sounds and for their parents' capacity to translate those needs fairly quickly despite not being formally trained in "facial recognition" or the habits of their new baby. Before our brains intellectually identify an emotion, our bodies start signaling us about it—an increase in cortisol, dilated pupils, and elevated blood pressure, for example, warned us in prehistoric days to be afraid when we detected the presence of a predatory animal.

Our bodies have the ability to assess situations and relay messages about them through emotions that we experience as physical sensations. Plainly put, it is our sixth sense or natural superpower to feel one another's emotions as though they were contagious. As humans, we have cells in our brains called mirror neurons that fire when we sense the emotional state of another, creating an echo of that state in our own minds.

Somatic or emotional empathy might come easier with people we are very familiar with, as we have more data to pull from to translate what we're feeling into a cognitive inference about the emotions that might be at play.

With time and practice, this ability to attune to another person's inner world is a powerful tool for persuasion, caregiving, and even friendship and romance. There is danger, however, that might be found in professions like medicine, the military, philanthropy, and education, where individuals are consistently faced with the emotionally charged and traumatic situations of their patients, clients, students, and beneficiaries. In these situations, too much emotional empathy, without appropriate boundaries and coping mechanisms, can lead to high levels of stress, anxiety, depression, and burnout. Sometimes this is referred to as "empathy fatigue" or "compassion fatigue." Individuals who

are at high risk for empathy fatigue and burnout must work to cultivate a healthy detachment and seek support to help keep that detachment from becoming indifference.

Affective empathy, or compassionate empathy, refers to having a strong grasp of both cognitive and somatic empathy and being able to separate ourselves (our ego) from individuals or situations to make an assessment about what might be required to support someone in a particular moment. With affective empathy, the individual is gathering information from their somatic response as well as their cognitive knowledge and using it to make evolved choices.

Affective empathy assumes no emotion is good or bad and that we are all connected through our emotions. As we detach from judgment about the emotions unfolding in a situation or with a person, we can actively listen, connect, and use what we are learning about the emotions to ensure our response has the appropriate emotional quality. Let's take anger, for example, which is often a signal that we are feeling disrespected or the need to protect, and can show up physically as heat, tension, increased heart rate, or even loss of cognitive ability. When a person we care about experiences and expresses anger, we might be moved to take action to affirm their feelings or to speak or act in their defense. Alternatively, let's look at sadness. A doctor might share challenging news about a patient to their family and feel their sadness. However, to join them in their sorrow with tears would be wholly inappropriate. Affective empathy requires that we channel our attunement and understanding, but then make a detached assessment about the most compassionate and constructive way to respond.

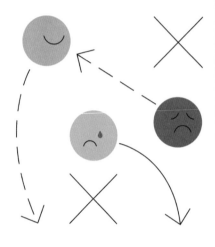

Most highly influential leaders are adept at this type of empathy. Think about a coach who calls a time-out during a tense moment in a game to calm the players down, outline a plan, and delegate roles. In this case the coach is using situational awareness, separating personal emotions from the intensity of the moment, and making a choice to pause and slow down with the goal of affecting the team's ability to execute.

One goal of this empathy journey is to heighten our understanding and application of affective empathy in our individual lives, homes, places of work, and communities. For our Day 3 exercise, I invite you to reflect on times you've witnessed each form of empathy. We'll use ourselves, our past experiences, and our history to strengthen our knowledge and awareness of each form. This way, we can enhance our ability to tend to our needs and ambitions and to deliver greater impact in the lives that we touch.

DAY 3

Exercise 1:
Empathetic Leaders

Think of three people in your life whom you consider to be particularly empathetic leaders. Write their names on a piece of paper, then answer the following prompts:

What makes you see this person as an empathetic leader? List three examples.

Which form of empathy do they use most often (cognitive/somatic/affective)? List three examples.

Exercise 2: Self-Assessment

Which type of empathy do you use most often (cognitive/somatic/affective)?

Think of a time when you have exhibited each type of empathy:

Cognitive Empathy
(Intellectual understanding)

Somatic Empathy
(Felt/emotional understanding)

Affective Empathy
(Empathetic action)

Write down your examples on a piece of paper.

Feelings Roulette Body Scan

What's something that triggers fear in you? How does your body respond to that fear?

When humans experience moments of fear, our nervous systems enter a fight, flight, freeze, or fawn state. We might more commonly refer to these fear-induced reactive emotional states as excitement, anticipation, anxiety, or panic. It was in one of these very moments, where my body went into freeze with no imminent danger in sight, that the idea of somatic empathy crystallized in my mind. Moments of fear are prevalent, making it a good place to start strengthening your attunement to somatic experiencing (how our emotions show up in the body).[10] On Day 4, I'll share how somatic empathy entered my life and prepared me to face some of my most challenging moments.

I was first introduced to the concept of somatic experiencing indirectly through a men's emotional leadership training and support organization called EVRYMAN, which I began to attend in the fall of 2018. My "men's group" grew out of EVRYMAN. Men's groups are a form of support or group accountability and nonclinical therapy that is becoming more prevalent across the world. The mission of EVRYMAN is to "connect men more deeply to themselves and others." Generally, they are rooted in a practice of emotional, mental, and physical exploration and self-discovery around trauma and the need for healing. I joined a group of six other men, led by several members who had met at an EVRYMAN retreat, training, or social event. I learned through this group that more than 80 percent of violent crimes are committed by men. This is just one statistic that stood out while I was exploring how men deal with emotion, myself included.

---

10. Crystal Ott. "What Is Emotional Intelligence?," Ohio State University Extension, last accessed November 14, 2022, https://ohio4h.org/sites /ohio4h/files/imce/Emotional%20Intelligence%20 Background.pdf.

At the time, I was in a rough space in my life. My business was running out of money with no clear prospects of how we would generate new revenue. My business partner was my then girlfriend. The love and enthusiasm we had for each other, along with luck and momentum, fueled our passion and creativity. Yet, our relationship was unraveling. We were having frequent fights—at times of an explosive nature. The defensiveness and anger that arose as an attempt to cope with uncertainty and unaddressed sadness in my life soon exacerbated the critical state of our relationship and business. Eventually, I would be unable to shake the sadness and resentment I held about my life situation. I didn't have this awareness then, but I was consumed with shame and the fear of failing. I was suffering, not fully knowing the extent of work needed to be more connected and loving to my partner.

As I look back on those days, I can still feel the shame I harbored deep in my gut. Today, when memories from that time resurface, I allow myself to feel that pain as intensely, or even more so, than I ever did. Back then I numbed the shame and withdrew from my family and my partner. So today, in order to accept, heal, and learn from my mistakes, I allow myself to feel the pain that I didn't have the self-awareness to notice or the tools to endure on my own. I share this example because shame over falling short of expectations is something most of us can relate to, and through examples from our own pasts we can examine how that memory shows up in our bodies physically.

Those days, the feelings of fear, shame, sadness, and anger were much more prevalent than that of joy. At that time, absent the self-awareness to notice that I was avoiding the feeling of desperation brought on by my entanglement in a failing business and rocky romance,

"The key to empathy is listening with curiosity."

I found solace in avoidance and toxic coping mechanisms. Though I was resistant to the concept of being in a men's group at first, an early benefit was that it gave me a weekly routine and provided a community of men I was able to trust to be compassionate mirrors for me.

It was through the group that I was able to express my true emotions in safety: tearful sadness, rageful resentment, buckling shame, unexpressed fear, and reticent joy. I began to accept that I did not know how to connect with, experience, receive, integrate, and constructively act on my emotions. No one ever told me that all emotions—joy, fear, anger, shame, and sadness—are safe and reveal valuable information about our needs and desires. Until I met those six men, no one had ever told me that my fear, my anger, my sadness, and my shame were healthy to experience.

The key to empathy is listening with curiosity rather than with predetermined expectations or judgments. It's listening with our ears, our eyes, our minds, and our hearts. Before joining the group, this concept was very foreign to me, but it began to take hold in practice before it made sense to me rationally.

Each group begins with a check-in ritual including a moment of mindfulness, like a few deep breaths or a meditation, followed by a slow and intentional physical and emotional audit from each man. Each man acts as a coach, encouraging the others to stay with emotions rather than detailed thoughts or stories. It took a while for me to truly begin exploring the idea that all my emotions, even the difficult ones, offer information. Today, my emotions tell me more about my problems and the way forward than I'd ever imagined possible. That is the power of empathy, and somatic empathy in particular.

Of the three types of empathy, somatic is perhaps the least practiced form—consequently, the one that most people are unfamiliar with and have trouble grasping. In Day 6, we'll dive deeper into the origins and science behind somatic empathy, but for now I invite you to start the way I did: Learn through your experiences. Begin by developing trust for the wisdom hidden in your own body.

It's said we store memories in our bodies. Joyful memories, yes, but memories of trauma in particular. When we experience situations that remind us of traumatic experiences from our past, it might generate a sensation, an emotional trigger ranging from subtle to inhibiting, as we experience the physical manifestation of this subconscious emotional response.

Think of a time that you've seen something suddenly approach in your peripheral vision, or when you were called on to speak unexpectedly. Usually there is an emotion that

manifests physically. A gasp of breath, a quickening of your heartbeat, a shift in awareness that makes you more or less alert. These are examples of how our bodies might react to feeling startled or surprised.

Whatever our natural inclination or regular activities expose us to, it affects our emotional reactions to similar stimuli. For example, a race car driver might have less of an emotional reaction to something approaching in their peripheral vision, just as a talk show host might have less of a reaction to being called upon suddenly to answer a question.

By deepening your ability to listen to your body through mindfulness, you can start to map your own particular emotional language. The exercise we'll practice together today works in much the same way. The Feelings Roulette Body Scan is a mindfulness exercise we've developed to strengthen our somatic empathy muscles. It allows you to experiment

51

with, learn about, and adapt to your emotional triggers. The exercise asks you to focus on and identify your physiological responses to stimuli (delivered in the form of reflective questions) and to connect those responses to one of the five core emotions. If you are coming into this book with an established mindfulness practice, you might find that taking notice of your somatic experience isn't difficult at all. No matter where you begin, there is always more that we can learn and explore.

Various mindfulness exercises encourage or enable greater connection to the body and the information it stores and communicates. One goal of this book is to leave you with several new exercises and modalities that organically integrate more mindfulness practices into your life, without requiring much effort or time investment. By the end of today, you will have added several mindfulness exercises to your wellness and empathy practice. You are already on your way!

52

DAY 4

Exercise:
Feelings Roulette

As you begin this exercise, deepen your breathing (deep inhales and slow exhales) and bring your awareness to your body. Whatever you are feeling after three deep breaths should be considered your baseline. Scan your body and take notice.

1. Scan your body for physical sensations and write down what you feel.

2. We've provided a list of questions for this exercise, along with a diagram to help you scan your body for sensations. When you read a question, restrain yourself from using your cognitive mind to answer it, and instead scan your body for any physical sensations or change. Some common reactions might be a change in temperature or a sharp reaction or tension in a place like the chest, shoulders, or abdomen. Take note, as these sensations

are likely to be similar to sensations you feel in other day-to-day situations.

3. After writing down the physical sensations, try to assign emotions to the sensations using the five core emotions you learned on Day 2 (joy, fear, shame, anger, sadness).

Question One: What did twelve-year-old you want to be when they grew up?

Question Two: Who was your childhood best friend? Where are they now?

Question Three: What is one trait you're proud to have inherited from your parents?

Question Four: If you could redo one moment in your life, which would you choose and why?

(Note the physical sensations on paper first, using the following diagram to help you locate them. Then label the sensations with joy, fear, shame, anger, or sadness.)

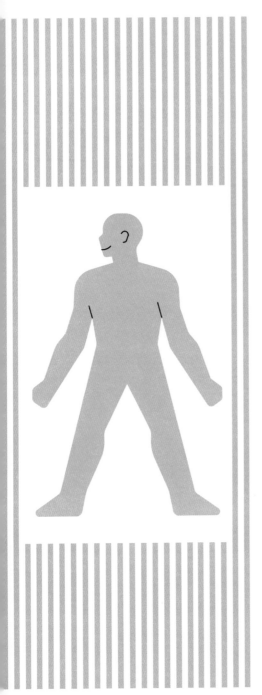

This is the most important tool of the power of empathy: the ability to notice our emotional reactions as they show up physically in our bodies. At any moment, we invite you to slow down, bring your awareness inward using your breath, scan your body for reactions or tension, and begin to get curious about what that sensation might be trying to communicate.[11]

11. To continue practicing Feelings Roulette, I recommend using the Actually Curious Happy Hour edition, which offers fifty-two introspective questions that help us explore the people, places, and ideas that bring joy. Combined with the Feelings Roulette exercise, it helps identify areas in our lives that bring us joy so that we can bring more attention to them.

DAY 5
One Day Mindfulness Challenge

What is your ultimate form of self-care?

Whether you came to this with an active self-care practice or not, our goal is to use empathy to strengthen your ability to support yourself and others. As the saying goes, "You can't pour from an empty cup." By prioritizing your own self-care and need to recharge, you are more equipped to approach people and situations with patience, attentiveness, and compassion. Across the past four days, we've laid the foundation for strengthening your empathetic abilities by establishing a shared language and teaching a few basic tools. On Day 5, we explore the idea of empathy as a mindfulness practice. Together we'll practice using mindfulness to listen to our inner voice and wisdom, by slowing down and tapping into all our senses and emotions.

At the mention of *mindfulness*,[12] for many people meditation is what comes to mind first. Meditation is one of the foundational practices of mindfulness, but it can also be a deterrent to those who are skeptical or just beginning. The paths to mindfulness are as varied as we are—they include walking, cooking, swimming, fishing, listening to music, writing, dancing—the list goes on.

Before I began my deep exploration of empathy, I'd dabbled in mindfulness activities like exercise, journaling, using saunas or steam rooms, and various forms of meditation techniques, including conscious breathing, positive visualizations, and body scan meditation. However, it wasn't until the summer of 2019—three months

---

12. *Mindfulness* has been defined as "a mental state achieved by focusing one's awareness on the present moment, while calmly acknowledging and accepting one's feelings, thoughts, and bodily sensations, used as a therapeutic technique" (University of California, Santa Barbara, Health and Wellness, "Mindfulness," https://wellness.ucsb.edu/challenges/happiness -challenge/ucsb-happiness-challenge/happiness -challenge-mindfulness).

into a romantic and business breakup, and when my brother Christopher passed away—that I managed to assemble these activities and more, as part of my self-care and mindfulness rituals.

That moment, losing my brother Chris, shattered the container holding all the work I'd been doing to move on, heal, and learn from the breakup. I thought all was lost, as my brother Chris was the person closest to me. Even as I write this and revisit the moment, I can feel my upper abdomen activated and the chest area around my heart constricting. My body remembers.

I'm reminded that during that weekend I found my will to live shaken, and my sense of self missing and exposed. I was alone in my New York City apartment. An apartment that had seen four committed romantic partners come and go. I was in the East Village, a neighborhood long since vacated by my close friends and peers, who'd moved on to start families or to find a slower life. I was alone in the apartment where my brother and I had hung out, where he had lauded me for the life I was creating for myself.

That weekend, after my family members and I had consoled one another over the phone, I found myself panicked and desperate. I turned to drugs and alcohol to escape the pain. But it only made my anxiety and depression worse. I paced back and forth, with my body temperature rising, my jaw clenched, my heart beating so hard that I could see it moving my chest through my shirt when I looked in the mirror. I called my ex-girlfriend Aaliyah, with whom I'd shared the longest of my relationships, and thankfully she agreed to sit with me and keep me awake until I sobered up. I was afraid I was going to overdose that night and knew I needed support. That weekend I had reached my rock bottom.

"Procrastination was my way of coping with the fear of failure."

Overcome with sadness and grief, fear and panic, shame and despair, I knew that I needed to channel everything I had into changing my habits. My first instinct was to dive into work to ensure my team was prepared for the period of bereavement I would take for a few weeks to support my family and make the funeral arrangements for Chris. Just two months prior to the loss, I'd been hired as the chief marketing officer of a nonprofit organization focused on social media and community-based health interventions—mental health among them. I was afraid to lose my momentum and standing on the job.

I had no clue what I was projecting and presenting in that work setting. After a few frantic meetings, I received a call from the CEO mandating me to take bereavement immediately. I had hoped to use work as a distraction, and I felt that my agency was being taken away. I can remember the anger and shame, and my throat constricting as I protested with as much tact and composure as I could muster. Looking back, I can see that my attempt at masking my emotional state was thinly veiled at best. My cognitive abilities were understandably impaired. My ability to stand out at work was an anchoring characteristic of my self-worth, and now even that was in danger.

Prior to this life-changing moment, I had a variety of habits that I now recognize as toxic, that at the time were simply ways that I blew off steam or things I did to survive. I was what one might call a weekend warrior. Throughout high school and college, I procrastinated during the week and weekend, only to cram in my work the night before it was due or I had a test to take. Procrastination was my way of coping with the fear of failure. Throughout my twenties and into my thirties, I worked long and intense hours at work, often capped by drinks with coworkers or friends. I'd perhaps take a night or two off before doing it again and partying even more intensely on the weekends. Between work, and dating, and getting drunk and high with friends, I had no time to truly examine my insecurities, inadequacies, and traumas.

That Monday following Chris's death, I started to brainstorm all the healthy ways I could use to distract myself from the grief, regulate my emotions, and put myself on a path to acceptance and healing. I reached out to my therapist, but with my appointment a few days away, there was little she could do for me. I felt isolated and angry—at my therapist, at the system, at my ex-partner, and at pretty much everything else.

I had learned through previous hardships to channel my pain and anger into longer runs than I was used to, which gave me a boost of confidence in my darkness. So I started there. I went out into the East Village, down First Avenue, and across the Williamsburg

Bridge into Brooklyn. I was shouting expletives and allowing the angry tape looping in my mind to run until I wore myself out. The angry loop tape eventually stopped.

I ran all the way north through Brooklyn to the Brooklyn Bridge to make my return to Manhattan. I began connecting again to sadness for the loss of my brother, dodging tourists with tears running down my face. As I made my way back up FDR Drive, joyful memories entered my mind, and I let out a euphoric yet tearful laugh. I found a spot in the grass in East River Park, right around Houston Street, where I stopped. It was a place I'd taken my brother before, and even some lovers in the past. It was a slice of peace and love for me. I sat in the sun and meditated.

When I returned home, I pulled out my journal and wrote and wrote and wrote. With the same freedom of experience I had welcomed on the run, I found myself yelling and cursing, my hands at times moving frantically, ink ripping through the fibers of the page with aggressive anger. At other moments, words slowly glided onto the page in a lyrical trance. Writing, an activity that I'd engaged in since I was a child learning to pass the time when I was bored and alone, gave me solace when I was grieving. A therapist once told me that writing allows you to externalize emotions and see them, observe them as they change. The idea had never stuck until now, when I so desperately needed to write through my grief.

During that week of bereavement, I did this routine of exercise, meditation, and journaling every day. Sometimes I'd do it twice a day. I was on leave for almost three weeks, so I had more time and spaciousness than ever before to solely focus on my family and myself.

Something was working during this period of extreme self-care. While the sadness over the loss of my brother still visits me today, I was able to identify and experience my emotions more fully. I wasn't numbing them like before. I was developing a better, healthier relationship with them. Emotions are like waves. They build to a peak, then they crash. My journaling helped me see that life cycle from start to end. I learned that emotions do not intend to stay; they only intend to grab your attention for a time. And during this challenging period in my life, I discovered that I could experience my emotions and not only survive but heal, grow, and thrive.

With this breakthrough with my emotions, even after experiencing more hardship, I never hit rock bottom the way I had after I lost Chris. My internal narrative had shifted from "Why me?" to "Resilience is a core part of me." I contemplated what living the rest of my life with a moment-to-moment awareness of my emotional and physical well-being might be like.

"Emotions are like waves. They build to a peak, then they crash."

I had been living outside of alignment with my integrity and purpose. In fact, I realized that I didn't have a clear vision of my intrinsic purpose, though I advised businesses on identifying theirs. So I began to make an audit of all the things that brought me joy and contentment, emotions that I struggled to channel easily. I was mapping out a unique path to happiness that was solely defined by me.

Months later, this exploration of intrinsic happiness would become my calling. Now I could channel the sadness from losing loved ones toward becoming better at loving myself. I got the idea that perhaps I could help others reach these revelations without hitting an emotional rock bottom first. I could be a model for others and share inspiration, knowledge, and tools to anyone who needed it.

As I progressed, I took notice of the connection between my body, my emotions, and my mind. My body would tell me things about my emotional state and needs, which informed the narrative in my mind and the ways I acted to satisfy them. Conversely, I began to see how narratives from my past about self-worth and about trust and safety were coloring my emotions and manifesting in destructive actions and habits. I became increasingly curious about how much I was missing by not slowing down and observing my emotions instead of being swept up in the waves until I crashed.

Three years later, I still keep a daily routine of exercise, meditation, and journaling, though I usually constrain it to an hour in the morning. I will proactively take a day off from work or other activities to extend that self-exploration if I find my concentration waning, my composure weakened, or my clarity in question.

* * *

The power of empathy is that it connects us to the present. Our expectations, our judgments, our fears, our ambitions—those all sit in the past and future, at times guiding us in a healthy way, and at other times getting in the way of the joy we could be experiencing in our precious minutes and days. If we can develop an internal muscle memory to actually be with our emotions, then we can hone the ability to act constructively with the good and bad that we experience. Let's get that muscle growing together. Judgments that get in the way of a mindfulness routine include not knowing where to start, wanting to do it "right," or thinking you need training or guidance. There are many ways to kick-start and enhance a mindfulness practice. I suggest you start with something that you love. Perhaps that's reading or taking a bath or making a meal. If it shifts your emotional state, brings you peace, and allows you to observe how you feel without judgment, then throw that activity into your personal mindfulness tool kit.

DAY 5
Exercise

On Day 5, open a note in your phone or a page in your journal and add observations to it throughout the day. Every time you notice a physical sensation tied to a situation or thought, think about what emotion goes along with that sensation and jot that down too. Remember, some common signals or triggers include loss of clarity in your mind; a change in body temperature; a sudden or lingering feeling of tension, constriction, or stress; or a noticeable change to the expression on your face. Think of this exercise like a real-life "feelings roulette," where instead of questions as the stimuli, it's the situations you organically encounter throughout your day. This exercise is about tuning your instinctual memory to be aware of the emotions present in yourself and noticing how they shift in response to even the smallest stimuli. If you find the open-endedness of this task a little daunting, here are some guiding questions that can provide you with a loose framework you can use throughout your day:

MORNING:

How do you feel first thing in the morning when you wake up? What physical sensations are present? What emotions are present? Does this affect how you wish to approach the day?

BEFORE THE START OF YOUR WORKDAY:

Before you start your workday, what physical sensations are present? What emotions are present? Does this affect how you wish to approach your work?

THROUGHOUT THE DAY:

As you encounter individual people or groups, what physical sensations arise? What emotions do they introduce or produce in you? Does this affect how you approach this person or group? As you move through your day, what memories surface? What physical sensations are present as you reflect on them? What emotions do these memories evoke? How do you want to honor, be with, or release these memories?

AT THE CLOSE OF YOUR WORKDAY:

When you arrive home, or even as you are preparing for bed, what physical sensations are present? What emotions are present? Does this affect how you wish to conclude your day?

These prompts are meant to get you going. If you feel something physical or emotional, don't judge it—write it down and allow yourself the space to examine it with an open mind to see what lies beneath the surface.

BONUS:

As a bonus assignment, share your biggest takeaway from the day with someone you care about who you think may benefit from your example.

65

The Importance of Intention

Goal setting has always been a way of being for me. But in the past, my goals were often driven by the expectations of my parents, or by the fear-based comparisons I'd become accustomed to making—to my siblings, colleagues, class-mates, and even celebrities I would see on TV, in maga-zines, and on social media. But losing my brother and going through a breakup with my romantic partner left me hun-gry for answers and healing. In the face of this uncertainty, I was able to feel grounded by engaging in a deep and intentional assessment of my values and how they react to my somatic experience.

Now, being intentional and living with intention aren't mutually inclusive. Engaging intentionally is similar to attunement. It means you aren't distracted or attached to a particular outcome. You are present, doing your best, and ready to receive what happens with curiosity. Living with intention means we aren't going through the motions. It's living with accountability to people, commitments, goals, and most importantly, to one's own desires and well-being.

As an ambitious person and avid self-learner, I explored many personal development and growth books through-out my twenties and thirties that introduced ideas around fear, human nature, and how we get in the way of our own progress. It was from Seth Godin's *New York Times* best-selling book *Linchpin: Are You Indispensable?* that I discov-ered the concept of the "lizard brain," a metaphor for how our amygdala and will to survive can at times get in the way of the decisions we should be making. The lizard brain is not merely a concept. It's real, and it's living on top of your spine, fighting for your survival. But, of course, survival and success are not the same thing . . . The lizard brain is the reason you're afraid, the reason you don't do all the art you can, the reason you don't deliver projects on time when you are capable. The lizard brain is the source of the resistance.

I was a middle manager at an advertising agency when I read that book, trying to learn and shape my own style of leadership. I began to observe how fear seemed to speak up at stressful times and result in frantic behavior, changes in plans, and a waterfall of stress for all involved. This appeared to be the norm in every place I worked and with most leaders I worked with. It was rare that I would be met with a sound plan or briefing. When I did, those plans and briefings rarely held up all the way through to the end of the project.

Little did I know at the time, but my outward judgment was a reflection of my own uncertainty about what I was doing with my life and why. In psychology, this occurrence is referred to as projecting. Most of us do it. Some of us do it more than others. In *Emotional*

Intelligence at Work, Jeremy Marchant explains projection as a term, introduced by Sigmund Freud in 1895, meaning "a symbolic process by which one's own traits, emotions, dispositions, etc. are ascribed to another person."[1] The definition explores a relationship with emotional discomfort related to self-awareness and assessment. *Psychology Today* adds to this meaning with: "Unconscious discomfort can lead people to attribute unacceptable feelings or impulses to someone else to avoid confronting them. Projection allows the difficult trait to be addressed without the individual fully recognizing it in themselves."[2]

I, like many humans, sought to prove my worth through my chosen employment. My path to happiness was to climb the

67

---

1. Jeremy Marchant, "Projection," *Emotional Intelligence at Work*, 2007, http://www .emotionalintelligenceatwork.com/resources /projection.

2. *Psychology Today* staff, "Projection," *Psychology Today*, last accessed November 9, 2022, https://www.psychologytoday.com/us /basics/projection.

corporate ladder and accrue material achievements. In my early thirties, I found myself overworked, often misdirected, seldom heard, and increasingly unhappy. I felt my leaders were creating conditions and giving direction that was affecting my well-being and made me feel neglected and inefficient. I would join coworkers and friends in lamenting the lives we'd created, avoiding our sorrows through drinks and dating and other ways of partying and forgetting about the workday.

It would be some time before I saw my judgments as a mirror of my own lack of clarity, an inability to be with my own difficult emotions, and responsible for the choices that affected my happiness and well-being. Despite convincing myself that I needed these jobs to give me safety and security, my choice to exchange my time and energy in ways that were out of alignment with my values and inner knowledge was actually exacerbating my suffering.

Around 2013, I read Simon Sinek's *Start with Why: How Great Leaders Inspire Everyone to Take Action*, which gave me a framework for my own business strategy and point of view. According to Sinek,

The struggle that so many companies have to differentiate or communicate their true value to the outside world is not a business problem, it's a biology problem. And just like a person struggling to put her emotions into words, we rely on metaphors, imagery and analogies in an attempt to communicate how we feel. Absent the proper language to share our deep emotions, our purpose, cause or belief, we tell stories. We use symbols. We create tangible things for those who believe what we believe to point to and say, "That's why I'm inspired." If done properly, that's what marketing, branding and products and services become: a way for organizations to communicate to the outside world. Communicate clearly and you shall be understood. (159)

"The key to strong motivation is to understand why individuals do what they do."

I was introduced to *Start with Why* by a dear mentor by the name of Chuck Welch. We partnered on a volunteer program introducing our colleagues and clients to culture thought leaders who were shaping the tastes and sensibilities of the youth, a novel concept at the time in mainstream media advertising agencies. Prior to taking a job as an integrated content producer at Publicis's Starcom, I had been working for two of the foremost brands in youth entertainment, MTV and Vice media, and had a natural eye for culturally resonant ideas. Chuck noticed a creative and strategic mind worth nurturing and took me under his wing. He encouraged me to get to the core of why I, and any brand I represented, did what we do. The key to strong motivation is to understand why individuals do what they do.

Chuck and I came together because we had several values in common, and together we made the larger agency establishment pay attention and

fund initiatives they otherwise wouldn't have. We were two of the few Black men in leadership roles at the agency. We both came from trendsetting cultural agencies and wanted to bring more of that energy to our traditional media agency. (Chuck was a part of the strategy team that led the partnership between the rapper Busta Rhymes and the liquor brand Courvoisier that gave birth to the song "Pass the Courvoisier." The song put the liquor brand in the center of hip-hop culture for the next decade. Chuck and his team understood a core connection between the love many in the Black community have for Cognac, hip-hop music, and fun times.) We both approached our jobs with a competitive edge and energy and were willing to put in extra work and hours to bring about something that was reflective of our beliefs and views of the world. We were compelled by several shared whys.

This approach, understanding the why before moving forward,

would soon become an anchoring principle for everything that I did. Each time I found myself stuck in my life or career, I'd find a comfortable place of solitude to reflect on why a certain outcome was important to me. I might set aside time to explore my why. I might go to a sauna, steam, and reflect at the East Village Russian & Turkish Baths or the Korean spa in New Jersey, alternating hot and cold treatments until I was out of my thinking mind and into my subconscious, and I could receive messages from my heart.

You might say I was "seeking the meaning of life" or trying to "find myself." Often these moments of deep reflection followed nights of partying, or weekends escaping in a short-lived romance. They might follow a stressful string of weeks where I put in extra duty at work most nights. I was searching for ways to feel happy, successful, and safe—to be a respectable man and

eventually a father. Amid my toxic escapes, I was slowly learning to endure the discomfort of asking deeper questions about what I needed in my life.

Around 2018, a year after I'd channeled the courage to leave corporate advertising and branch out on my own, I read *The Laws of Human Nature* by Robert Greene. I was seeking inspiration on how to be a better leader and desperately trying to bring direction to Curiosity Lab. The book was the biggest contributor to ratifying my curiosity on how understanding human nature might help me find my own happiness and lead others to theirs. *The Laws of Human Nature* draws from the ideas and examples of Queen Elizabeth I, Martin Luther King Jr., and many others to teach us how to detach ourselves from our own emotions, master self-control, and develop the empathy to look behind people's masks, resisting conformity to develop our purpose. In Greene's words,

Learn to question yourself: Why this anger or resentment? Where does this incessant need for attention come from? Under such scrutiny, your emotions will lose their hold on you. You will begin to think for yourself instead of reacting to what others give you.[3]

When we live in accordance with our values, it not only affects our well-being but also who we surround ourselves with, how we allow ourselves to be treated, and how effectively we pursue our goals. In Phase Two, the Importance of Intention, we explore how knowledge of our values helps us move our emotions into actionable information. We'll begin to examine how our values translate into our pursuits and our defined or undefined purpose in life, as well as how the perception of our values is influenced by outside elements, like our families, schools, places of work, and popular and community cultures. Ultimately, we'll learn to create safety and security within ourselves by using our values and emotions. These tools will support us in building trust for ourselves that incrementally grows to become the trust we foster across our communities.

3. Robert Greene, *The Laws of Human Nature* (New York: Viking Press, 2018), 21.

DAY 6
Somatic Experiencing

How does fear relate to your biases and to the systemic imbalances present in society?

This is a big question. Systemic imbalances refer to systems and structures that have procedures or processes that intentionally disadvantage African Americans and other under-privileged and under-resourced groups. I suggest unpacking the question using the tools and knowledge you have already learned. First, how does the question make you feel? Where does the feeling show up in your body? Was it one dominant sensation, several, a wave? How would you label the emotions this question brings up—joy, fear, anger, shame, sadness? Now that you've learned to ground yourself, remain present and acknowledge your emotional response to this challenging question. Go ahead and answer. Read your answer and think about how it compares to what you would have written had you not slowed down into your somatic experience first.

Day 6 has already begun! Today we'll explore how somatic awareness, in service to our core values and purpose, can be used as a legend for translating feelings and emotions into messages from our inner voice.

I was in a Starbucks parking lot the first time I distinctly noticed the connection between the sensations in my body and a shift in my emotional state. Donald Trump was president at the time, and I felt fear and panic after seeing a God Bless Our President sticker on the back of a white minivan. I noticed this response echoed how I feel when driving in the South or when I see Confederate flags or the bull bar of a highway patrolman, and I recognized that this feeling was my body's way of reminding me that, in this moment, I was presented with a possibility of danger just because of the color of my skin. The clenching in my jaw, chest, and throat and my increased heart rate were physiological warning signs to be careful. By bringing my awareness to what was happening to me, I was able to slow down the sensations of an impending panic attack.

That was Memorial Day 2020, and the next morning I awoke to news about the death of George Floyd, the Black man murdered by former Minneapolis policeman Derek Chauvin. The feeling of panic returned.

Driven by that sense of urgency, my partner Caroline and I decided to use the Actually Curious Instagram account and email, as well as my own individual platforms across Instagram, LinkedIn, and Twitter, to raise awareness and encourage action to improve the protection of Black and brown people in America. Our why for doing this was that feeling of panic I had experienced traveling the country just months prior—a feeling that many Black and brown people live with in this country: the fear of being presumed guilty or assumed to be a threat instead of being seen as an ally or an asset. The correlation of that tragic day and the panic I experienced the day before catalyzed months of work to define my unique purpose and how I would direct it. My why was to create a world where people like me could feel safe.

We began using the platforms at our disposal to facilitate the difficult but necessary conversations about the conscious and unconscious biases that led to George Floyd's death. I used my values at the time—curiosity, grace, resilience, leadership, and consistency—to translate my fear into speaking up and gathering others to join me in amplifying my message.

In the example I just provided, I used somatic experiencing to make sense of a particularly distressing situation. However, making a ritual out of somatic experiencing can have therapeutic benefits. A regular practice of somatic experiencing can shed light on what is actually happening in our bodies when we experience emotions at any point.

Somatic experiencing, or SE, is a form of psychotherapy developed by therapist Peter A. Levine aimed at treating trauma and PTSD. Clients track their physical experiences in professionally guided sessions. The primary goal of somatic experiencing is to rewire reactions to trauma-related experiences. To do so, an individual's attention is directed to internal physical sensations first, rather than trying to solve or make intellectual sense of the traumatic experience.

What I uncovered is that somatic experiencing can also work to bring clarity and keep us in line with our intentions, as much as it can be used to confront trauma that is hidden beneath the surface. We will use somatic experiencing in this way later in the book. If you suspect that you may benefit from using these methods to uncover unexplored memories and trauma, I invite you to discuss somatic experiencing with a therapist or coach as soon as you can. Until then, try somatic experiencing in these daily exercises and in your life, and listen to your own inner voice with pride.

DAY 6

Exercise: Somatic Experiencing

To close out Day 6, let us explore somatic experiencing using some difficult but important questions. As you explore them, pay attention to what physical sensations arise. Experiment with iden-tifying what emotions you would asso-ciate with those sensations and why. Then answer the questions and reflect on how the awareness of your somatic response has affected your answers.

1. What fears or traumas have you inher-ited from your parents or ancestors?

A. What physical sensations arise as you contemplate this question?

B. Which of the five core emotions would you associate with your physical sensations?

C. How has your awareness of your somatic response influenced your answer?

2. How did the election, pandemic, and protests of 2020 impact your life?

A. What physical sensations arise as you contemplate this question?

B. Which of the five core emotions would you associate with your physical sensations?

C. How has your awareness of your somatic response influenced your answer?

3. How do you love?

A. What physical sensations arise as you contemplate this question?

B. Which of the five core emotions would you associate with your physical sensations?

C. How has your awareness of your somatic response influenced your answer?

4. Describe one time that you've judged someone based on a perceived difference.

A. What physical sensations arise as you contemplate this question?

B. Which of the five core emotions would you associate with your physical sensations?

C. How has your awareness of your somatic response influenced your answer?

77

Intrinsic vs. Extrinsic Values

Name someone from your childhood who was significant in shaping who you are today. What makes you think of that person?

It's usually the people we love and respect that come to mind when we reflect on this question. Our parents and grandparents, teachers, siblings, and coaches. People who nurtured us and provided safety. Our role models, those of us who are fortunate to have them, help form our values and our view of the world. Also among our influences are our peers, schools, and places of work. Even the societal and popular opinions of our respective generations play a part. On Day 7, we'll expand our knowledge of our values. We'll examine how outside sources and influences impact individual values and beliefs. Our goal is to learn how to use empathy to get curious about which of our motivations are extrinsic and which are intrinsic.

Intrinsic motivations are ideas that bring clarity and joy for their own sake. Intrinsic motivation comes from within, without any ostensible external rewards. Behaviors that are internally motivated are done because they are inherently enjoyable, and not because of any anticipated reward, deadline, or outside pressure.

Extrinsic motivations refer to ways of being that are concerned with what we get as a result of our actions. Extrinsic motivators are the external rewards that drive some of our behaviors. For example, many of us stay in a job longer than we want to because the salary is a strong extrinsic motivator.

Both intrinsic and extrinsic motivators play critical roles in our survival and in our happiness and ultimately help inform our held values.

Our values are important drivers of our ambitions and passions, our beliefs and fears. They influence whom we date, which professions we pick, and even what car we drive or neighborhood we choose to live in. Some of us have clear and intentionally defined values. For others, values may be more intuitive—gut instincts that guide us through difficult moments and help us make quick decisions. (We will come to learn that we all have this power.)

Through my own journey into empathy, compassion, well-being, and grace, I've learned to observe all values with curiosity and kindness. I've learned by having grace for myself. My mistakes, my accomplishments, my delayed rewards, and my primal desires. All values are a part of our learned codes and unconscious responses to the worlds around us. By understanding our values as intrinsic or extrinsic, we can make conscious choices about our behavior. Today, I have much more awareness of my values, and I'm therefore better able to act with integrity.

These days, driven both by social media and rising demands for accountability, it's become the norm to answer for our values. This has been important in bringing about change and exposing those who have abused their power and access. This transparency and pressure to display our values has also increased stress. It heightens the expectations that we all must live up to. I'm here to help you navigate this new normal and to support your peers and family in doing so, too.

Back in 2019, the combined events of my business failing, my relationship failing, and then losing my brother Chris ruptured my sense of self. I had to learn to rebuild from within to find the strength to carry on. I did survive. And from those dark moments, the value of resilience started to take root in my subconscious. Born from the need to soothe myself when I was young and often playing alone, curiosity was another value that brought me peace. Curiosity in work, in friendship, and in love. I needed to know that though I had stumbled, there were parts of me that I was grateful for. I was grateful for the explorations and risks I had taken that embodied my core value of curiosity.

These were my intrinsic values. Traits that I've had for a long time. Perhaps for my whole life. These traits would support me in my hardest times. I saw resilience and curiosity in my father and mother. Those values helped deliver them from their challenging beginnings on the island of Jamaica. My father, Ralton Lascels Peterson Tennant, immigrated to America when he was twenty-two on a trade visa. Orphaned at the age of four, he'd learned the trade of upholstery, and leveraged it to access a brighter future in America. He'd later buy his business and own it until he retired in 2012. He bought my childhood home in 1978 and sold it in 2012. He used his trade to put me and my brothers through school. I benefited from his hard work and from both my parents' investment of time and resources in my future.

My mother would immigrate later, and my brothers would follow. She explored various careers throughout her life; she worked as a maid in a hotel, a clerk in a record company, and a supervisor in an interior decorating company. Finally, she landed a union job within the New York City hospitals. That last career choice provided the pension and health insurance

"The value of resilience became my shield, and curiosity my escape."

that supports her and my father today in their retirement.

I have no doubt that my intrinsic values are influenced by my parents. My siblings, the tough neighborhood I grew up in, the books I read, and the television I watched made a contribution, too. My predominantly Black middle-school teachers reinforced important lessons about my Black history. They also warned me about my future as a Black man, and how the world might view me because of it. The value of resilience became my shield, and curiosity my escape.

A key part of my healing was realizing I needed to slow down enough to analyze my inner thoughts and narratives. I knew I didn't want to remain buried in grief. And with some awareness of how I wanted to feel, I noticed that my thoughts alone were keeping me mired in feelings of sadness, shame, fear, and anger.

While on bereavement leave, I chose to refrain from any form of avoidance or numbing. I'd sworn off substances, video games, TV, and the work that I'd normally thrown myself into. By doing so I created space to get deeply curious about the emotions that arose from moment to moment. I began to see how emotions could arise from perceived judgments from people I loved, from people I answered to, from acquaintances, from strangers, and even from myself.

My attachment to material belongings, like my $2,800-per-month apartment in the East Village, was rooted in extrinsic values. It embodied my pride in the prestige and history of the neighborhood and my attachment to my time there as a young adult. The shame I felt from losing my previous romantic partner and pausing the business of Curiosity Lab stemmed from perceptions of how our social circle saw us. I feared the envy I projected onto our peers for our love and our short-lived success. Noticing these extrinsic desires and motivations, I began to untangle shame and fear (real and projected) from what I actually needed and wanted for myself. I would need to turn to my family and peers for help as I navigated this fall from grace.

Even today, when I reflect on those moments, I can feel activation in my abdomen and in my chest, our centers of self-worth and love. I'm reminded that there were many extrinsic values, motivations, or possessions that I was then and still am willing to let go of. In my darkest hours, my inner voice identified another value: grace.

This isn't to say that extrinsic values are bad. When Chris passed, I stepped into a mediator's role, a facilitator's role, and a financial supporter role in my family, where situations where I had to lead were more frequent than I was accustomed to. To lead in the face of challenge and heightened emotion requires grace. My support for others would require money, which made me more mindful of the extrinsic benefit of a salary. I had to learn new skills for confronting shame, anger, fear, and sadness as I became more engaged with family dynamics and disputes. I began to have much more contact with the values and traumas of the people I held most dear, which sometime came into conflict with my own experiences. I can feel physiological signals of my own resistance rising as I write or reread this passage, reminding me to go slow. Our most difficult empathy work is often confronting the layers of protection we built up in our childhood homes.

Author Robert Greene explains that humans live disconnected from our intrinsic values and motivations. "We want to learn the lesson and not repeat the experience. But in truth, we do not like to look too closely at what we did; our introspection is limited. Our natural response is to blame others, circumstances, or a momentary

lapse of judgment."[4] The difficult emotions that arise when
we are beginning to be introspective is our nervous system
distracting us rather than
allowing continued contem-
plation. When we examine our
intrinsic and extrinsic values, we
gain a tool that helps us look
at our emotions with context
and safety. The grounded state
we aim to achieve through
willingness to experience the
arising emotions helps us
remain detached and curious
when we review the choices we
and others make. This practice strengthens our ability
to understand ourselves and
others, free of judgment.

83

4. Robert Greene, *The Laws of Human Nature*
(New York: Viking Press: 2018), 31.

DAY 7

Exercise

To practice, our Day 7 exercise invites
you to get curious about the origins of
your values. Accept as truth that outside
influences exist. Be patient with yourself,
as the process of noticing our outside
influences is hard work. Breathe into any
physical and emotional sensations or
discomfort. Do your best and have fun.
This relationship of self-reflection and
compassion is one you get to practice
for the rest of your life. Give yourself
limits and boundaries, like ten seconds
of reflection per value, and be prepared
to enjoy the ride.

Finally, I've found that this exercise can
have lingering effects. Be prepared
to give yourself five to ten minutes to
ground yourself before reintegrating others or returning to work or providing support. If this exercise brings up any difficult
or traumatic memories from the past,
seek professional or community support.

Select ten values from the following list that are important to you. Release any judgment, and do your best to identify ten words or phrases that are actually important to how you live your life and treat the people around you.

Now take about a minute with each word to freely journal about the external influences that might have contributed to your claiming this value—your family? Social structures like school or work? Or something else, such as a TV show or story you loved?

LIST OF VALUES*

Achievement
Adventure
Beauty
Calmness
Creativity
Fairness
Family
Freedom
Free Time
Friends
Fun

Honesty
Humor
Independence
Knowledge
Love
Loyalty
Morals
Nature
Peace
Popularity
Power
Reason
Recognition
Relaxation
Respect
Responsibility
Safety
Spirituality
Stability
Success
Variety
Wealth
Wisdom
... add your own!

---

*List from TherapistAid.com, 2012.

DAY 8
Exploring Our Values

What moral or cultural values do you hold in high regard and why?

The first time I ever actively contemplated my values was in my thirties. Long after I was introduced to values as a child through family, school, and church. Long after my awkward and insecure teen years. Long after I made choices about what to study in college. And more than a decade after I entered the professional workforce.

In the years since, I've learned that I'm not alone. Most of us are taught what we need to know in order to function and excel in society, but very little time is spent teaching us to understand ourselves. The goals I set for myself were often driven by a loose set of values that were shaped by the expectations of my parents, or by the fear-based comparisons I'd become accustomed to making—to my siblings, to my colleagues, to my classmates, and even to the celebrities I

saw on social media. I learned at a young age that if I didn't meet my parents' expectations, there was a good chance I'd be punished. I also learned that my performance would be perceived differently depending on how my brothers before me, or even my other classmates, performed. The schools I attended routinely used public displays of performance rankings as a reward and motivation tactic. Because academic achievement was externally motivated, and obedience and competition are not strong values for me, I'd have a difficult time maintaining my focus. My internal motivations didn't always line up with external motivations, which made it hard for me to determine whether I was on the "right" path. If a career that was in line with my interests, for example, wasn't yielding me the same monetary success as my college friends', I'd question whether I'd made the right choice.

My first true deep dive into assessing my values was

alongside my team at Curiosity Lab in 2018, less than one year into founding the company. We had found a niche working with purpose-driven companies like the Swedish oat milk brand Oatly and the salad company Sweetgreen. We asked them what their values were, audited how well they delivered those values to their consumers, and offered recommendations for how they could do even better. But as we were preparing to onboard our interns in the summer of 2018, we realized that we couldn't clearly articulate our own values to them. A brief moment of shame washed over us when we realized that. We were advising companies on how to improve the very thing we, ourselves, were struggling with.

We took this opportunity to practice what we had been preaching, and to strengthen our connections to one another. We decided to start with a demonstration of transparency and vulnerability by exploring and discussing our individual values together first, before exploring the values of the Curiosity Lab as a cohesive and trusting collective. What unfolded was an experience in self-reflection that created lifelong bonds between relative strangers. But perhaps the more meaningful discovery for me was the new tool that I had gained. I'd always found time for introspection, but this values exercise gave me a process for auditing and assessing or reassessing the values that matter to me at any given moment. The values exercise would become a foundational anchoring tool in my work and my life.

Something about exploring my values just made sense. I developed a ritual where I'd create the space away from my partner, away from family and friends, and away from day-to-day responsibilities to revisit this exercise and reassess my values. Back then I did this a few times a year, whenever I felt unsure about my direction and goals. Over the years, as hardship has led

"It became clear to me which spaces deserved more of my time and energy."

me to greater connection to who I am—the good and the bad—my inquiry into my values has become more resonant. I might see a word out in the world and know, through a strong physical response in my body, that this is a value I need to pay attention to. As I gained this greater connection to my values, it became clearer which places and spaces I needed to be a part of or remove myself from. It became clear to me which spaces deserved more of my time and energy. The more I knew my values, the easier it also became to confront self-limiting narratives like "I'm not good enough to be loved" or "People won't invest time, energy, or money in me because I am Black."

When I learned to deeply connect to my inner or intrinsic values, I began setting goals that would make me happy, regardless of the success or esteem they might afford me. I'd heard the phrase "Do what you love and the money will follow" hundreds of times before,

but the idea had only partially stuck in my mind. I separated my happiness from the expectations of lovers, family, friends, and employers, and my values informed how I set boundaries and goals, which helped me find happiness from within.

A values exercise is similar to an exercise you perform in athletic training: You start off learning the basic mechanics, but the real breakthroughs and enjoyment will happen after you've done enough repetitions. It may take a few tries before you arrive at your most deeply resonant values. It may take days, weeks, or even years to master.

Day 8 is about exploring and identifying deeply resonant values and using them to craft your purpose statement. Identify a space where you'll be free from distraction for thirty minutes. To begin, practice taking three long deep breaths, followed by three slow exhales to bring your focus into your body. The key to identifying deeply resonant values is creating the

89

conditions to connect deeply with yourself and the emotional feeling or physical reaction evoked by the words that will become your values. I know I've found a resonant value when I experience a shift in my body. Like a change in temperature, tightening in my chest or abdomen, a smile on my face, or even tearing in my eyes. Our ability to notice our somatic response helps us to identify words that matter to us.

On the next few pages, I've included the steps of an exercise to guide you through identifying your values and crafting them into a purpose statement. I invite you to use what you've learned about somatic experiencing as a foundational tool and amplifier in this exercise.

For the best effect, read each prompt one at a time without skipping ahead. This will allow the exercise to help you remain present in your emotional experience of the words, rather than defaulting to the intellectual experience of picking or explaining. And here's a pro tip: There is something special about exploring values by hand, so I invite you to pull out your journal.

Your journey into intentionally connecting to your values and purpose begins today. Who's to tell what magic you will soon create as you strengthen your self-awareness, expand your willingness to experience, and discover clarity of purpose? I, for one, can't wait to find out.

DAY 8

Exercise: Values and Purpose

1. From the following list, select all the words that resonate with you as potential core values. Don't overthink it; just highlight, circle, or write down all the words that you feel aligned with.

Abundance
Acceptance
Accountability
Achievement
Adventure
Ambition
Appreciation
Attractiveness
Autonomy
Balance
Being the Best
Benevolence
Boldness
Brilliance
Calmness
Caring
Challenge
Cheerfulness

Cleverness
Collaboration
Commitment
Community
Compassion
Consistency
Contribution
Cooperation
Creativity
Credibility
Curiosity
Daring
Dedication
Dependability
Diversity
Empathy
Encouragement
Enthusiasm

Ethics
Excellence
Expressiveness
Fairness
Family
Flexibility
Freedom
Friendships
Fun
Generosity
Grace
Growth
Happiness
Health
Honesty
Humility
Humor
Inclusiveness
Independence
Individuality
Innovation
Inspiration
Intuition
Joy
Leadership
Learning
Love
Loyalty
Mission-Oriented
Motivation

Open-Mindedness
Optimism
Peace
Perfection
Performance
Personal
  Development
Power
Preparedness
Proactivity
Quality
Recognition
Relationships
Reliability
Responsibility
Responsiveness
Risk-Taking
Safety
Selflessness
Service
Simplicity
Spirituality
Teamwork
Thankfulness
Thoughtfulness
Traditionalism
Uniqueness
Usefulness
Versatility
Vision

2. Group all the words that you've selected in a way that makes sense to you. Create a maximum of five groups of similar values. If you have more than five groupings, drop the one that feels least important. Don't overthink it—there are no right or wrong answers, just what's right for you.

3. Once you've organized your groups, pick one word from each group that you believe represents the label for the entire group. Again, there's no right answer here. Just consider what feels right to you.

4. Now we're going from saying to doing. Add a verb to each value so you can see what it looks like to make a value actionable. For example: Growth—Accept growth; Mindfulness—Be mindful.

5. Place your actionable values in order of priority for you. At the top should be the value that you feel is your biggest

93

priority; at the bottom, the value that you feel is the lowest.

6. Turn your core values into your unique purpose statement. For example: Driven by a pursuit of clarity, I've thoughtfully prioritized my values so that I can live in my purpose.

DAY 9

Living Through Your Values

What do you think you could become famous for?

We don't all want to be famous, but most of us do want to enjoy the things we spend most of our time doing. Whatever your dream, ambition, or vision for contentment might be, your values and purpose statement will ensure that you achieve it. Your purpose statement is only valuable if you use it, so let's put it into practice together. Now that we know our values, let's bring them intentionally into our choices, large and small. On Day 9, I'll invite you to use what you've learned about somatic experiencing to have the first of many intentional conversations with your inner voice.

One of the most valuable lessons I learned along the way was that I had much greater agency than I ever realized. I had the ability to identify the things that mattered to me, and to use them to shape my choices. Knowing my values and purpose statement, and having a more attuned awareness of

my body, helped me clarify my desires and my boundaries.

The road to becoming an empathy expert was neither simple nor easy. Even today as I write this book, I have to make trade-offs of time, energy, and attention that require checking in with myself daily. Today, taking time to check in with my emotions, my intentions, my family and community, and my actions has become second nature—but I had to create this ritual and make it a habit.

It's important to note that the ritual that works for me may not suit you completely. The thing that made this process stick for me was anchoring my mindfulness and check-in ritual around things that I already enjoyed. Let mindfulness become a part of your play and self-care, while working on your values and purpose becomes an investment in yourself and the things you care about most.

The thing that makes this practice of empathy so valuable is that it provides a blueprint for showing love and compassion to oneself, from the inside out. It assumes that if you are connecting to your most intrinsic calling, you will more clearly navigate to your own unique sense of happiness. You will also have enough emotional capacity to share your skills with your community. Although this is not the focus of this book, you will likely unlock greater material success in a more fulfilling way, as well. The key point there being "more fulfilling."

Fortunately for me, my self-empathy ritual came to me as a lifeline. In the week following my brother Chris's passing, I took space by heading to a local sauna and steam house. It is important to incorporate things you naturally do to relax into your self-empathy ritual. For years I'd used saunas and steam rooms to detox after partying, while also getting my mind into a trancelike state of relaxation and reflection. There I spent the afternoon, about three to four hours, doing an extended assessment of my values and purpose.

After arriving at a deeply embodied purpose statement and set of values, I began to revisit my statement daily in my journaling sessions. Each morning, I'd wake up and intentionally refrain from using my phone for social media or email. I'd freshen up a bit by brushing my teeth and washing my face and then proceed to meditate.

At this moment in time, I would use the Insight Timer app, a library of timed meditations, and meditate in silence for twenty minutes. About a year prior, I had been trained in a self-guided meditation by the 1 Giant Mind meditation program, led by Jessie Israel. So, practicing in silence works for me, but it takes experience for most. A simple guided body scan meditation would be my recommended place to start for a beginner.

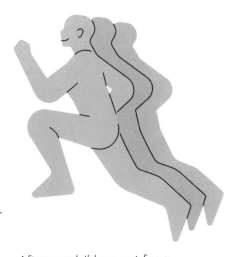

After my meditation, I'd pull out my journal, write my purpose statement at the top of the page and then begin to write.

I had ample time to slowly journal because I was on bereavement leave. I'd read each value out loud, monitor the reaction in my body that day, and freely write about that. I had a lot of pain, anger, sadness, and resentment from my loss—and those emotions interacted with my values and came out in words. Sometimes those words were dark and other times poetic. I was able to express the entire spectrum without judgment.

Afterward, I'd go out for a run. My brother died largely because of poor health, so though I wasn't in a similar health situation, I wanted to run to model for myself what it might take to stay away from a similar fate. While on those runs, I'd become fatigued, and I'd hear my purpose statement creep in. "Born from curiosity and resilience, I find the strength to lead with grace." The words *resilience*, *leadership*, and *grace* would mix with the anger in my heart to send more blood and more energy outward into my limbs and my brain. I'd run for a mile or two longer!

Those runs were my longest and fastest runs ever. While I was running, the values were at work. Something about mixing physical movement with an intentional practice of checking in with my emotions and thoughts made the intentions more firmly rooted in my psyche. I began to clearly see how to heal, how to show up, how to support, and how to thrive. My purpose statement helped transmute my sadness and anger into physical energy, and the physical movement helped me turn my purpose statement into positive and actionable ideas and thoughts.

For the almost three weeks that I was out of work to support my family, I'd incorporated yoga, a bike ride, or even a long walk into my physical movement routine, always bringing my purpose statement along with me for the ride. I observed how it interacted with the world around me and noticed that it showed up in my judgments, choices, sensations, and expressions. My purpose and values started to become an organic part of my day-to-day life. Now it's time to imagine what living through your values and purpose might look like for you.

As with all our lessons and exercises, my goal is to share ideas and a framework that you can make your own. Earlier, I described how I recovered from my brother's death in 2019 by introducing a ritual of mindfulness, exercise, and responding intentionally to stimuli. I now invite you to do the same.

This routine will help you establish a consistent and intentional relationship with your emotions and how they show up in your body. It is useful for seeking more clarity of purpose and optimizing and amplifying the joy your days bring you. Our ambition is to achieve a sense of direction that originates from deep in our souls. A sense of clarity that guides us to invest our time, attention, and energy into experiences that are intrinsically impactful and meaningful.

DAY 9

For our Day 9 exercise, I invite you to use what you've learned about somatic experiencing to have a conversation with your inner voice. Take your purpose statement from Day 8 and write it below or at the top of a blank page in your journal. Underline the values in that statement. Then reflect on a series of questions that I'll offer to you, using all your senses and your purpose statement as inspiration. Practice going through the progressions, from body, to emotions, to thoughts. Then bring the learnings you received from those reflective questions, like anchors of safety and building blocks of imagination, to help you envision the future of your dreams.

WRITE YOUR PURPOSE STATEMENT:

THINK OF THE THREE PEOPLE YOU SPEND THE MOST TIME WITH; WHAT DO THEY ALL HAVE IN COMMON?

Body:

Emotions:

Thoughts:

WHEN DO YOU FEEL MOST FREE?

Body:

Emotions:

Thoughts:

WHAT DOES "PERFECT" MEAN TO YOU?

Body:

Emotions:

Thoughts:

WHAT IS ONE THING YOU WOULD CHANGE ABOUT THE WAY YOU WERE RAISED?

Body:

Emotions:

Thoughts:

BONUS: YOUR CHECK-IN RITUAL BRAINSTORM

What is the best time of day to get thirty to sixty minutes of movement and reflection? Morning, afternoon break, after work, before bed?

What are things that you'd enjoy including in your ritual? Some ideas include a cup of tea, yoga or stretching, tarot cards, or Actually Curious questions.

How will you get into a meditative state? Some ideas include taking three deep breaths, listening to a meditation, or going for a mindful walk.

Relying on Your Values

What wish do you have for humankind?

One unifying truth among us is that we will all experience the loss of a loved one or soulmate one day. I chose sympathy as my wish for humankind, because after I lost my brother Chris, I began the journey of experiencing what the death of a deep love and soulmate would feel like. Until this point, death hadn't hurt this bad. It helped me understand the pain others go through. I also chose perspective, because that loss changed my life in such a dramatic way. I became a more resilient, focused, thoughtful, and determined person on the other side of the pain. On Day 10, I'll teach you how to use your values as a core anchor for navigating loss, healing, and support. We'll start from empathy for self to strengthen our abilities to achieve our deeply felt wishes for ourselves and our communities.

My family losses began to pile up between the months of December 2018 and October 2019, beginning with the passing of my uncle John in December, my aunt Cindy in March, and my brother Chris in July. These losses were a crash course in learning the stages of grief, and they would prepare me for one more loss in October that tipped me deep into life and belief change. The change that inspired my social justice, entrepreneurial, and spiritual transformation. I believe my story was able to inspire many people because it happened around the same time that many others were experiencing loss. As of the writing of this book, more than one million people in the United States and more than six million people worldwide have lost their lives due to COVID-19.[5] Even more drastic might be the sheer number of people who have experienced a significant break in their lives, routines, and relationships as a result of the global pandemic and

5. World Health Organization staff, *WHO Coronavirus (Covid-19) Dashboard*, last accessed November 9, 2022, https://covid19.who.int/.

concurrent military conflicts—most public among them being the war between Russia and Ukraine. All breaks carry significance, and we grieve them in ways that are similar to how we grieve the people we lose through death.

I learned two big things when Chris died. The first is that grief can stop us in our tracks and significantly change us. While my initial instinct was to spring into action to leave my colleagues prepared for my absence, it turns out that I was also attempting to escape through one of my validation sources—my job. My behavior became slightly manic, without me realizing it. My speech on calls, the energy I brought to interactions, it was all strained. I needed an extended bereavement leave of absence from work to heal myself and to focus on my family.

The other thing I learned was that people will rally around with support when someone is grieving. Perhaps it is because many have experienced loss already and know what it's like to go through it. Or perhaps it is a part of our natural human instinct to offer empathy and sympathy. When I lost Chris, I thought I would be forced to ask for help and support in a way that was new to me, but instead I didn't even need to ask. People from all walks of life were willing to reach out and hold space for the pain that I was working through. It was as though a community of angels came to support my healing. It was a glimpse of an abundance that I didn't know I had or needed.

Beyond the external support, there was a lot happening internally as well. I didn't know this then, but there are both psychological and biological patterns around grief that are helpful to be aware of when experiencing loss of any kind, or when trying to intentionally provide support. According to a *New York Times* article entitled "The Biology of Grief":

First is a shock in which you feel numb or intensely sad or angry or guilty or anxious or scatter-brained or not able to sleep or eat or any combination of the above. During those first weeks, people have increased heart rates, higher blood pressure and may be more likely to have heart attacks.[6]

Death and grief can create a ripple effect that affects our mental and physical well-being, creating negative outcomes if we aren't able to heal appropriately. The article references a particularly acute effect of grief among spouses; over their lifetimes, according to studies done mostly on bereaved spouses, they may have a higher risk for cardiovascular disease, infections, cancer, and chronic diseases like diabetes. Research on bereaved parents and spouses shows that within the first three months they are nearly two times more likely to die than those not bereaved, and after a year, they are 10 percent more likely to die.

Those first few moments upon learning of Chris's death felt like a bomb went off in my head and my heart. It was an instantaneous break in my internal reality and psyche. Being Chris's little brother was a huge part of my identity and sense of safety. And what made my grief particularly acute was that I was also going through a breakup and tackling my substance abuse in therapy. Chris was my main pillar of family support.

I'd shared with Chris my truth around addiction and had even gotten his support when revealing this shame-inducing reality to my mother and father. He helped keep the peace in that conversation and offered my parents some perspective about how anger or shame would make my recovery harder. Chris, who had experienced a stroke in 2016, had experienced his own deep loss,

6. Ann Finkbeiner, "The Biology of Grief," *New York Times*, April 22, 2021, https://www.nytimes.com/2021/04/22/well/what-happens-in-the-body-during-grief.html.

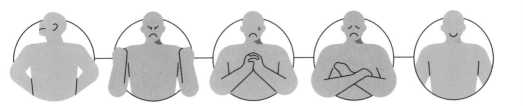

as he had been living without full motor abilities in his left side. I was deeply inspired by the shifts he'd made in the aftermath of his stroke. Humbled by the loss of physical ability and grateful for his second chance, he was making strides with physical therapy and modeling a sense of grace and acceptance, while becoming more emotionally reliable. You might say that observing his grief and healing gave me a point of reference for what healing from a deep loss could look like. Eventually, you have the option to accept and move forward with what you have.

I shared with Chris an observation that was emerging from my therapy appointments and efforts to heal from my breakup; I'd come to learn that I relied on my romantic relationships as sources of my happiness. The external validation that I received from the emotional and physical connection with my romantic partners provided an ephemeral sense of accomplishment. They made me feel connected to the values and ambitions that I admired and coveted in or shared with them. My romantic relationships were a part of my identity, and I was deeply grieving my most recent loss. Chris was my biggest support in that process, and then he died suddenly. With those two losses happening so close together, I was left feeling broken.

Although my recovery was drawn out and intense, it also followed the five stages of grief fairly closely: denial, anger, bargaining, depression, and acceptance. At first I sprang into explosive sadness, filled with questions about why this was happening to me and my family.

For help, I reached out to my ex, looking past all the reasons we had broken up three months prior. I assumed that she would support me through Chris's death, but instead I found myself crossing her physical and romantic boundaries and resenting her need for distance from my grief. It would take me years to really understand the situation, but at the time I moved into anger. Anger at her, the doctors, my brother's wife, my parents.

As I began to contemplate the role I'd need to play in the family to fill the gap from his loss, as well as how to hold it together after the breakup, I began to search for ways to make the pain and loss meaningful. Psychologists call this bargaining. I needed to negotiate a reason why all the painful moments were happening and figure out what I could do to make it right. Really, I was looking for ways to move through the pain and into actions that would perpetuate his memory. This is where I began to turn to my values. As I was still in a confused and disoriented state, my values gave me a structure that allowed me to check in with what might lie beneath my heightened emotions. They also gave me a lens for processing those heightened emotions and deciding on my actions.

Emotions are powerful. The somatic response to the emotions that arise out of grief can literally shorten our lives. Grief is a very powerful force that can do harm, but I've also found that it can inspire good. Imagine, if instead of toxic energy eating away at our bodies, you could transmute that energy into productivity. I didn't know it then, but that is exactly what was happening as I journaled through my values.

"I saw the pain and how it catalyzed differently depending on the person."

When I lost my brother, the fabric of my family's existence shifted dramatically. I saw the pain and how it catalyzed differently depending on the person. I witnessed my parents losing a son. I witnessed two nieces and a nephew losing their father. I witnessed a spouse and friends losing someone they loved deeply. All suspended in time, because really, I was absorbed in my own undecipherable grief as well.

Every day of those first two weeks was unpredictable. After having an argument with my brother's former partner Allison, where I commented on something personal to her, I left feeling ashamed of how I handled our relationship. That important relationship was now strained, a sign that I had to grow beyond the triggering arguments that pervaded our family and into being able to instead address pain and conflict with grace. I was so consumed by my grief, and in the reading I was doing

around mental health, that a comment I made triggered a strong defensive response that caused distance between us. It was as though I had a cognitive understanding of what she might be going through, but my use of that knowledge was far from effective. When I look back, I only saw myself as a grieving brother. I didn't see her as a grieving former partner and parent. I wish I had held more space for her loss of one of her best friends and the father of her daughters.

One day following this incident, as I was searching for answers, inspiration, and direction, I pulled the Actually Curious question "What gift would you share with humankind?" Answering through the lens of my values—my purpose statement at the time was, "Anchored in curiosity and resilience, I find the grace to lead with consistency"—I realized I had much more ease with the aspirational values of grace, leadership, and consistency. I was also learning to give myself grace more consistently. The statement and values were doing their job—internally and externally—preparing me for the future challenges that would lie ahead.

It was in moments of reflection like this that I developed the belief that if I could model the vulnerability to share my story with my family and community, I could make my healing meaningful. I could use it to illustrate the process of healing and the connection that could arise from it. A year later, the larger public would start to take notice of this movement around understanding and compassion for collective healing.

We all experience moments of heightened emotion, good and bad. The more we know about the power of emotions, how they affect our mind and our bodies, the more we can work with it to achieve well-being, belonging, and happiness. Grief is a part of life. When it does arrive, know that your own healing is crucial to your survival, as well as to your ability to support anyone else in your life.

DAY 10

Exercise

On Day 10, I invite you to transmute heightened emotions by exploring the question that brought me so much focus and inspiration: "What is a wish I have for humankind?" Before answering the question, think about how your values might help you make a contribution to your community. Channel the power of your unique gifts to this universe. Remove all editing and judgment. Check in with your heart, your body, and your mind, in that order, and then in random order. And then write your answer.

Be connected to your inner voice.
And have fun.

Channeling Purpose

Over the past two phases, we've established a shared and expanded understanding of empathy. Phase One: The Language of Feelings helped us understand the relationship between emotions and behavior, while Phase Two: The Importance of Intentions showed us the link between empathy and our beliefs and perceptions. We've learned exercises that strengthen our ability to use empathy to listen to, make sense of, and act on our inner voices. It's now time to turn our newfound knowledge into muscle memory. When we feel safe and grounded in ourselves, we can take risks and expand our aperture for how we use empathy within our communities. We can begin to channel our purpose and make an impact on the world around us.

By channeling purpose, you are establishing empathy rituals that direct your emotional awareness outward. You are, in effect, increasing your capacity for self-compassion—a key component of channeling purpose—which can have an enormous positive effect on your sense of happiness. And from the rituals you establish, the empathy that is discovered can unlock new possibilities in your relationships—from the personal and romantic ones to professional, family, and community relationships and, most importantly, your relationship with your own dreams and ambitions.

In Phase Three, we will deepen our base skill sets and expand our tool kit for self-compassion. We will begin to expand our awareness of the people and circumstances around us and notice the influence they have on our emotions.

Before we begin, I invite you to think about the people and places you interact with most and the situations that you actively avoid. What emotions come up? Joy, fear, anger, shame, or sadness? Treat these situations like the archives of your own life, which you get to examine and reexperience without judgment.

The key to self-compassion is viewing emotions without judgment. None are good or bad, but rather each one is a signal from our subconscious or inner voice about the situation at hand. Reviewing scenarios you've already lived through is a safe way to audit your emotional response. In Phase Three, we'll spend time slowly and intentionally reflecting on past experiences to unearth clues that can support us in our lives ahead.

We'll practice proactively finding sources of discomfort and invite them to teach us rather than pushing them away. This may sound intimidating at first. Even as I write this concept down, I can notice the muscles in my biceps tensing up. My back is becoming a bit stiffer and more strained. My neck is straightening and seemingly locked into place. My body appears to be

preparing for a battle. I can use that information.

With practice, I've learned what my body does when preparing for danger. In this case, the battle is against an internal fear that I may encounter something that I'm not expecting or that I'm not prepared for by examining my past. As you practice the language of feelings and importance of intentions with patience and regularity, you, too, will begin to translate physical responses into insights and direction with ease.

We each carry our own unique experiences. A situation that might be easy for me to encounter may be terrifying for you. I may be avoiding something that you would find enjoyable. Empathy, as we are exploring in this book, is about developing a thirst for unpacking all emotional responses with curiosity rather than judgment. Together, we'll practice attuning our awareness and willingness to feel. We will unlock new skills that help us understand what we need to heal and grow.

Judgment and compassionate observation cannot exist at the same time. This is most true with ourselves. We cannot judge something about ourselves and love it at the same time.

We cannot scorn our pain—our sadness, our fear, our shame, our anger—and heal from it at the same time. If we dismiss those feelings rather than accepting them, we never get close enough to the origins to end the ripple effect that these emotions produce.

We cannot reject the emotions that arise within ourselves and genuinely hold space for those same emotions arising in others. It is difficult to endure pain in others that we aren't yet equipped to recognize and be with within ourselves. Your ability to cultivate self-compassion is critical to quieting your own ego and to opening your awareness to the perspectives of others.

Regardless of the situation, you can learn to default to curiosity about your emotional response. You can use your sense of purpose and values to inform how you act on emotions. Together, we'll model using daily experiences and interactions with others to strengthen our empathy, understanding, and compassion. We will strengthen individual resilience and create greater capacity and momentum toward the impact we want to leave on the world. We will leave our communities and the world so much better off than the way we initially encountered them.

Circles of Control and Influence

What is standing in the way of your happiness and radiance?

Today, we examine our routines and our interpersonal connections. We'll review their alignment with our values and set new intentions for our self-development. By auditing where we spend our time and energy, we can establish a ritual that helps us channel our energy into the pursuits and connections that bring us the most joy.

We all have experiences we encounter or pursue for our growth and experiences we may choose to avoid. In 1989, author Stephen Covey wrote about how to confront these choices consciously and proactively in his bestselling book *The 7 Habits of Highly Effective People*. He demonstrates with three circles a way of organizing all the situations we face in life that take up our energy: the Circle of Concern, the Circle of Control, and the Circle of Influence.

For Covey, the Circle of Concern encompasses every situation and challenge we face in our work and in our life. This is the largest circle. The model asks us to assess and make choices about which of the situations and challenges in that large designation belong inside our Circle of Control.

Many situations—like the weather, the pandemic, the economy—are out of our control. They affect us, but worrying about these greater forces is ineffective and draining—it gets you nowhere. Other situations, such as how we respond to people, our performance at work, and our diets, are totally within our Circle of Control.

There are also things in our Circle of Concern that we can't control directly, but which we can still do something about. This is our Circle of Influence. We actively expand our Circle of Influence when we take action within our Circle of Control, instead of waiting for

"I was addicted to experiencing intense emotions of fear, anger, and sadness."

things that are out of our control to happen.

This practice Covey describes, of assessing what we control, releasing the concerns that are out of our control, and strengthening our confidence when responding to personal and professional situations, also applies to the Five Phases of Empathy outlined in this book.

An important skill to master on our journey toward empathy is responding to emotionally challenging situations that matter most in a grounded, productive, and positive way. A big step to doing this confidently is learning which situations require protecting or managing our energetic investment. These situations, in essence, would exist within our Circle of Influence.

I had a major breakthrough on my personal journey when I learned that the biggest drags on my happiness were situations I chose to say yes to almost automatically. When people in my family or friend

circles were in pain, for example, without conscious thought, I would say yes to listening without setting any boundaries. This put me in a position to not only share their trauma, but also re-trigger mine. You might say I was addicted to experiencing intense emotions of fear, anger, and sadness, over and over again. It was truly a misery-loves-company situation. My willingness to commiserate and stay focused on their trauma made me a great listener, but through this commiseration I was reinforcing powerful bonds to dark and negative past stories.

I had a habit of avoiding my past and the difficult emotions attached to it, which would result in another round of hangovers and recoveries that didn't actually solve the underlying issues. Too often, it was easy for me to say yes to other people's trauma or choose an outlet for my fears and frustrations, rather than examine my own behavior. When I learned that I had the power of choice—I could control my interactions with people—I became an active participant in creating boundaries around my happiness and energy. I stopped automatically saying yes to substance abuse or to losing myself in work, play, romance, or other numbing behaviors, allowing me to finally address my fragile emotional state. This understanding led to healing from the addiction, depression, and social anxiety that had prevented me from fully connecting to myself and others.

I recognized my misery-loves-company moments as a warning about a pattern of behavior. You might consider this moving my happiness out of the Circles of Concern and Influence and into the Circle of Control. I chose not to listen to the telling and retelling of someone's pain, if that telling resulted in further pain for both of us.

None of this work was easy, or without struggle. I eventually learned that for everything I say yes to, I say no to something else. The time and energy I choose to spend on toxic escapes is time, energy, and money that can never be recovered. It is time I could have spent with the family I'd lost. Time I could have spent in more intentional connection with friends and lovers. I've since learned that how I spend my time is one of the most important decisions I can make in my life.

Today, the freedom to make my own choices—both those that work for my life and enable me to be the most fully present and effective for myself and others and those that reflect my decision to protect my needs and feelings without fear of punishment or recrimination—stands among my most important values.

The choice to exercise this freedom often results in having uncomfortable conversations more frequently, but at least I know that I'm committing myself to environments and activities that bring me joy and safety. I've found that even though introducing my boundaries to people or organizations that may not be accustomed to them might cause some friction, other people are surprisingly willing to adapt. The vitriol that a boundary might produce in those who refuse to accommodate you can also be surprising, and often indicates a mismatch of needs and values.

I've learned the hard way that we can't be all things to all people all the time. We often can get so wrapped up in showing empathy and compassion for others that we forget to take care of ourselves in the process. We can get so caught up in the inertia of wanting to please and do a good job that it can cloud how well we are taking care of our own needs and priorities. This book is giving you permission and support to stop that pattern of behavior. If we want to ensure that we are channeling our energy to the places and spaces that matter most to us, we have to strengthen our ability to say no to situations and people that we encounter on a day-to-day basis that drain our energy.

For the givers and saviors out there, this will be hard work that inevitably leads to those difficult conversations that I mentioned earlier—conversations many people go to great lengths to avoid. This avoidance is often rooted in subconscious trauma patterns tied to shame and fear, and can be triggered by unhealthy power dynamics, low self-esteem or self-worth, or a history of unaddressed toxic or abusive behavior. Identifying and undoing this behavior can be challenging. Most people will not be able to flip a switch and acquire this level of self-awareness right away. In my case, my own individual work amplified the guidance I received from therapists and the progress I made through my men's group. These represented a choice to invest time and energy in spaces that would support my need for healing. I actively feed my Circle of Control with choices that are in alignment with what I want for myself, today and into the future.

As I've learned to have greater compassion for myself, I've begun to see that the way I feel is very rarely about the situation or people around me. When I'm able to slow down and approach myself and those around me with compassion, I realize that my emotions are often a result of my choices. The amount of rest I've had and what I've chosen to put in my body can have an immediate and noticeable impact. My integrity, which is how my choices align or misalign with my values, has a significant impact on my emotions.

Sometimes we fall short of our expectations to control our emotions or remove ourselves from trauma-inducing or shame-triggering situations. In these cases, we have three choices in our Circle of Control. One, having grace for missing our goals. Two, resetting expectations with ourselves or whoever is involved. And three, releasing and reframing shame-inducing paradigms and language. Instead of viewing a situation as "falling short," a negative framing that can lead to a trail of emotions that prevent us from bringing our full self to situations, we can express gratitude for the experience that will allow for better forecasting in the future and move on to other aspects that are within our control.

Once we reset our goals, give ourselves grace, and take time to rest, we attract greater collaboration, arrive at more creative solutions, and experience more fulfilling connections with others. We are human; we make mistakes. To that, I'll add we are human; we feel shame. Whether or not we let powerful difficult emotions like shame consume our thoughts, energy, and actions is 100 percent within our control once

"How we feel isn't always in our control, but how we react to our feelings is."

we strengthen our emotional awareness and regulation.

How we feel isn't always in our control, but how we react to our feelings is. This is the point. This is the Circle of Influence when it comes to empathy for ourselves. The more we are aware of our emotions, the better our ability to navigate them openly and collaboratively.

Beyond our personal challenges, the emotional qualities of community building and collaborative problem-solving are varied. Difficult topics surrounding growth, change, and healing are never easy to confront. But when we set intentions for our progress together, we are better able to endure whatever comes up. We accept this whenever we become deeply engaged in working and living harmoniously with others, but most of us do not have an infinite amount of energy to share. This is why it is important to take a step back and audit our energetic investments.

DAY 11

Exercise

On Day 11, let's identify the emotional quality of our relationships and make intentional choices about how and where we want to show up. This exercise will help you practice bringing greater atten-tion and energy to the places where you can make a gratifying impact.

Find a safe and inviting space to think about the people, places, communities, and activities that you spend the most time with over the course of a month.

Take three deep breaths to ground into your body. Focus your thinking on your past and day-to-day choices with love and compassion. Begin to imagine those people, places, and communities. We'll call these your "energetic spaces" or "spaces."

Take a page or whatever is needed and write as many of those spaces as you can imagine. This represents a vision board of all the spaces you spend your energy and time.

Narrow the list down to the ten spaces where you spend the most time.

Now narrow the list to the five spaces where you spend the most energy.

Of the five spaces, ask yourself the following questions:

How does this space make me feel?

Is the time and energy I spend here in line with my values?

What does my inner voice tell me about my purpose here?

Finally, revisit your vision board and identify any spaces where you wish to direct more energy.

Anchoring in Self-Love

If you could redo one moment in your life, good or bad, what would it be?

We all do this from time to time. We travel back in time through our memories, stopping to visit a moment that we want to cherish or perhaps pausing to experience a difficult loss or a regret that brings the feeling of shame. While our work in *The Power of Empathy* provides tools to help us all remain grounded in the present moment as we experience all of it, having a healthy relationship with our past is also important to our daily well-being. We carry the weight of moments left unexplored. That weight multiplies as new challenges and stressors enter our lives in the present. Our pasts are a part of us, and learning to love those past experiences as important parts of our individual journeys, good and bad, is one of the greatest acts of self-love that we can adopt. On Day 12, we'll introduce a ritual of using empathy to revisit our past to learn about our sources

121

of happiness, our triggers of discomfort, our motivation patterns, and our boundaries.

On an airplane, we're always told to put on our oxygen masks first before helping others. In life, many of us face difficult emotions such as shame, fear, or sadness when we attempt to put ourselves ahead of our children, our parents, our jobs, or our friends. In fact, as empathetic beings, putting others before ourselves can be a phenomenal source of joy and happiness. It might seem counterintuitive at first, but if we want to manifest more moments of generosity and joy, it's helpful to reflect on moments when our care for others has left us feeling depleted or less than ourselves. These are times when we might feel shame for falling short of our own or someone else's expectations, real or imagined.

Sadly, it's common to shame and to be shamed for things large and small. It's almost the norm to default to judgment of others and of ourselves rather than reacting with compassion to actions that defy our hopes or expectations. In childhood, it's common for a parent to react to a mistake with a disapproving look or reprimanding words, rather than a supportive gesture and reassuring words. But it's exactly that kind of forgiveness that fosters trust between people and gives a child the self-confidence to learn and try again. The same applies to many of the schools and teachers that have reared the current generation of adults, as well as the workplaces that provide financial security to our working population. So many of our systems and communities, religion included, freely wield shame as a means of enforcing group norms and agreements, and as a way of addressing and reprimanding mistakes. It's no wonder we barely notice it happening, let alone take a stand to protect our self-esteem from subtle attacks and our time and energy from being manipulated for another's benefit.

To practice self-love, we need to understand how and why shame plays such a dominant role in our society. In order to commit to vigilance against these subtle attacks, it's important to understand the powerful effect shame can have on a person's sense of worth and ability to lead a happy, healthy life.

According to philosopher Hilge Landweer of the Free University of Berlin, certain conditions must come together for someone to feel shame. Notably, the person must be aware of having transgressed a norm. They

"Our wounds affect us in subtle and powerful ways."

must also view the norm as desirable and binding because only then can the transgression make one feel truly uncomfortable. It is not even always necessary for a disapproving person to be present; we need only imagine another's judgment. Often someone will conjure an image of a parent asking, "Aren't you ashamed?" Indeed, we may internalize such admonishments so completely that the norms and expectations laid on us by our parents in childhood continue to affect us well into adulthood.[1]

This dynamic of parenting was certainly true in my home. It was common for my siblings and I to be strongly reprimanded using less than loving language. Today, we've come to understand this to be a form of emotional abuse. Back then, those hurtful words and even physical methods of enforcing rules and values were commonplace and generationally

passed down. I now recognize the long-term effects that verbal abuse had on my self-confidence and development, and I have even greater empathy for the challenges others face leading emotionally secure lives after surviving other forms of abuse, such as domestic violence or sexual assault. Our wounds affect us in subtle and powerful ways well beyond the actual moment of transgression.

Shame can cause people in need to isolate rather than seek help. In the days leading up to the death of my brother Chris, I'd been avoiding telling my parents about the struggles I was having in my romantic and professional lives. Before then, my parents had been critical—both directly and through subtle comments— of my decision to leave my high-paying corporate job in 2017, and to start a business with my girlfriend. Since childhood, my mother had expected me to marry a Black woman, and while my parents

123

---

1. Annette Kämmerer, "The Scientific Underpinnings and Impacts of Shame," *Scientific American*, August 9, 2019.

got along with my Caucasian ex-girlfriend, their disappointment was deeply ingrained in my mind, and at times present in their actions. Further, I'd only recently shared my struggles with addiction with them.

Given the facts that Curiosity Lab was foundering and my relationship had failed, in addition to the fear and sadness I was experiencing with the other challenges in my life, I was met with more possibilities for shame than I could handle. I spent a lot of energy staying away from my parents back then. Today, I'm much more secure in myself and my direction and am seeing the long-term benefits of the boundaries I've enforced with my family.

By learning to love and support myself, I was able to become deeply aware of my parents' patterns and develop compassion for them. That compassion helps me to remain grounded and lower my ego when their words cause me discomfort. When they scrutinize my choices, I remember that they were raised in a post-slavery, post–British colonial, and Christian-dominated culture in Jamaica where it was common to subject children to a kind of unyielding examination of their priorities. Domination is the only kind of rules enforcement they know. As a result, my parents raised me to fear disappointing them. If I did, I was met with shame and punishment. This may have had a fortuitous effect in some cases, especially in academic and professional settings where I was among the few people of color and perhaps exposed to more scrutiny and judgment than my white colleagues. But overall, anything I did that ran counter to their expectations would put me in a deeply unhealthy emotional place.

Today, I am much more grounded in who I am and what I individually believe in. Their words have less of an effect on my self-esteem, which allows me to focus on the relationship rather than the

"Shame teaches us we are not worthy of love and capable of improvement."

unintentional attack on my ego. It has also helped me establish clear boundaries for myself and enforce them from a place of love and compassion. Eventually, by understanding their past, I was able to learn how to maintain my grace in their presence regardless of what might be said. The results have gone beyond making visits more enjoyable—we actually have seen our confident modeling leave an influence on my parents' behavior toward us and toward one another. My partner and I, and our child, will benefit from the added time we'll get to spend with my parents as a result of my understanding of and growth through our relational patterns.

But let's be fair, my parents were far from alone. As I reflect back on moments of shame throughout my life, more instances arise. I remember teachers publicly celebrating the kids who performed the best in class, and publicly shaming the kids who hadn't performed "up to standard."

This method of teaching is rooted not only in the lack of curiosity for why some kids may not be performing as well as others but also in the complete disregard for the intrinsic gifts and superpowers that aren't measured by standardized testing, and that inadvertently become diminished by the public attacks on the children's esteem and worth. A child's ability to concentrate on, retain information about, and perform self-directed or time-based challenges is shaped by more than just their raw potential or lack thereof. Most environmental factors are beyond a young person's control. If we want to foster the gifts and potential of our youth, shaming tactics should never be an option. Shame teaches us we are not worthy of love and capable of improvement. I had to learn to default to self-love as the antidote to any time I felt shame. There is no progress through shame, and its use is so common that we don't even notice. Self-love helps me set a firm boundary for myself around

125

shame and model the same for others, no matter the short-term reaction my boundary might cause.

I was in my midthirties when I acquired the self-awareness and self-love to notice and set boundaries around shame. These new tools have helped me extend grace when my parents inadvertently slip into shaming tactics or when I encounter judgment in myself or as I interact with other people. It is this cycle of compassion that allows me to continually deepen my relationships with my parents, my community, and myself.

Don't get me wrong—shame has and does play a role in helping maintain social order and interpersonal commitments. In her article for *Scientific American* entitled "The Scientific Underpinnings and Impacts of Shame," Annette Kämmerer, a psychologist and professor emerita at the Institute of Psychology at Heidelberg University in Germany, puts it this way:

It has been speculated that humans feel shame because it conferred some kind of evolutionary advantage on our early ancestors. For instance, it can potentially promote a group's well-being by encouraging individuals to adhere to social conventions and to work to stay in others' good graces.[2]

We compete for spots at the top schools; for ranking in classes, hobbies, and athletics; for the best jobs and the highest salaries and titles. This book will compete for attention with other personal development books, social change books, books by Black authors, and so forth. We compete for attention, affection, love. Perhaps it's the fact that we are always in competition that makes it so important that we have a healthy relationship with ourselves and with shame. This is

2. Kämmerer, "The Scientific Underpinnings and Impacts of Shame."

especially true for groups that find themselves on the vulnerable side of power dynamics. Careful observation of systems of power reveals the subtle role shame plays in preserving the current social order and distribution of resources. For me, business maxims like "You have to pay your dues" come to mind. This phrase intends to shame ambitious individuals for expecting to advance too quickly. Or "Don't burn bridges," a phrase warning of the long-term ostracization that's possible if you cross someone with the power to affect your reputation.

Even when we have a healthy relationship with competition, we can find ourselves swept into the flow of it, living a life and making choices that take away from our integrity and well-being. I was certainly guilty of this. After high school, I held on to regret and shame for not getting accepted into my top choice schools. After college, I held on to shame and regret for partying too much,

for taking a while to focus and achieve good grades, and for distancing myself from my friend groups. In my adult life, the regret I felt for choosing a creative career rather than a career in more lucrative fields like finance would leave me comparing myself to my friends. Most of all, entering my mid-thirties and watching my peers settle down and start families left me with sadness and regret over my track record of failed relationships.

That weekend when my brother Chris died, all my regrets came to visit me. I questioned my own worth and will to live that weekend. Thankfully I was able to snap out of that downward spiral and anchor in the belief that I had a purpose toward which I could redirect my life.

My experience with self-esteem and shame mirrors academic research on the subject. Kämmerer notes in her writings that

in 2010 a team of psychologists led by Ulrich Orth of the

University of Bern studied shame in more than 2,600 volunteers between the ages of 13 and 89, most of whom lived in the U.S. They found not only that men and women manifest shame differently but also that age seems to affect how readily people experience it: adolescents are most prone to this sensation; the propensity for shame decreases in middle age until about the age of fifty; and later in life people again become more easily embarrassed. The authors see this pattern as a function of personality development. The identities of teenagers and young adults are not completely formed; in addition, people in this age group are expected to conform to all manner of norms that define their place in society. Uncertainty as to how to deal with these external expectations may make them quicker to feel shame. By middle age, in contrast, our character is more or less set, and norms have less impact. But as we enter old age and worry about declines in our body and our appearance, we begin to feel self-conscious again.[3]

An understanding of how shame affects us at various stages of our lives has helped me look back at younger versions of myself lovingly. My parents, who are now seniors, are still working to understand their use of shame and how it affects people. Throughout my life they had been models of self-assessment, which I absorbed as their child. And so my inner dialogue was colored by shame. It kept me from being present in my accomplishments.

I went to a prestigious college and was accepted to four out of the six schools I applied to. Shame kept me focused on imagined reasons for why I might not have been admitted to the two other schools, instead of celebrating the accomplishments of being accepted to college at the age of sixteen and

---

3. Kämmerer, "The Scientific Underpinnings and Impacts of Shame."

> ## "Life doesn't so much happen *to* us as it may happen *through* us."

becoming the first college graduate in my immediate family. There was so much more to celebrate than to feel shame for, but no one told me that.

In college, I was involved in music, campus activities, the Black and Latin Student Union, and Greek life, while studying economics, philosophy, and religion. Yet shame kept me focused on my lack of wealth compared to other students. Today, I celebrate my diverse studies for making me a well-informed and empathetic person, and I celebrate my social life for helping me become connected to culture, a key contributing factor in the success I've had in my entertainment and advertising career.

I am now grateful for the curiosity and rebelliousness that led me to interesting pursuits and adventures, rather than languishing in regret over not leading a more measured and conservative life. I get to live childhood dreams of creating and distributing a game to thousands of people, and I engage crowds through my talks and workshops. It took work to accept and love myself so that I could transform the patterns of shame and negative self-talk into levity and self-love. It was this level of self-love that unlocked my belief in new possibilities for myself and the resilience and consistency to follow through.

129

Through self-love we become aware of how our inner narratives affect what we pursue and what we accept. From this place of accountability, we can view the world around us through a different lens. Life doesn't so much happen *to* us as it may happen *through* us, as a result of our attention and choices. As I let go of the shame I was made to feel for honoring my boundaries while disappointing another person's expectations, I realize I'm a lot more accountable for what happens in my life than I might have realized.

For example, there will be times when we find ourselves overextended. A common pattern for me throughout my life would be to overextend myself in work, in play, in family, and even in love. In cases where our leanings toward generosity and compassion have left us feeling depleted, oftentimes a slight modification might make all the difference in our resilience. Perhaps I might need a nap, rather than allowing shame to lead me to tackle one more task or accept a last-minute invitation. Perhaps I might need to say no to a requested deadline and take time to propose a new one, rather than saying yes to a boss or colleague out of fear of shame or disappointment. Perhaps I might need to stop a friend or family member from continuing to vent, letting them know that I've reached my limit, rather than continuing to listen and growing resentful of their lack of awareness. Essentially, self-love is our guide for setting these boundaries.

With a greater awareness of our boundaries, we are better able to find space and recharge, ensuring that our tanks are full when we need them. But the self-loving, self-empathetic way isn't always easy. It often involves facing discomfort now for delayed gratification later. With practice it becomes muscle memory. A present and intuitive reaction to a physical sensation or an internal emotion translates into clarity about our boundaries and desires, then helps us make choices that contribute to our happiness.

One of the most resonant pieces of advice I received on my journey to healing was that everyone heals differently. I'll take that broader to share that we all experience differently. Often our moments of heightened emotion—fear, anger, sadness, shame, even joy—are informed by a deeper story hidden beneath the surface that shapes how we each respond.

DAY 12

Exercise

On Day 12, we commit to the idea that all emotions are good. They are like a best friend, here to help us see what's true, no matter how easy or hard it might be. Our emotions offer important signals to help identify when we need safety (anger or fear), or when we need to ground and recharge (shame or sadness), or when we are indeed recharging (joy) and want more. But first we need to learn to invite our emotions in without judgment.

1. For today's exercise, I invite you to ground deeply in your body and immerse yourself in this guided meditation. Bring your attention into your body by focusing on your breath. Take a few deep breaths, followed by long, slow exhales. Give your-self five to twenty minutes of intentional breathing and reflection based on your capabilities and need. Feel free to set a timer to help you keep track of time.

2. Set an intention for deepening patience, self-compassion, resilience, and grace.

3. Contemplate the following mantra for the day: I attend to myself with love.

4. Contemplate your values and purpose statement and how they relate to your boundaries and needs.

5. Repeat these words, "I attend to myself with love," to focus your awareness on self-love and to invite the lessons that come with sharing and enforcing boundaries.

6. Finish by giving yourself a smile, a hug, and a thank-you for coming to this place of self-love and awareness.

Repeating this simple love and kindness meditation will help you focus your awareness on your emotions and invite the lessons those emotions offer.

DAY 13
Challenging Your Beliefs

Who are the three people you spend the most time with? Why do you think that is?

Oftentimes the people we spend most of our time with say something about who we are or who we believe ourselves to be. This is because we surround ourselves with people who make us feel affirmed. Contrast this with when you ask a person to describe themselves. The answer often varies based on the context. But you may get a more telling response if you ask about who a person spends the most time with.

Who we are changes based on our mood, our stage of life, the company we keep, the company our company keeps, and so forth. On Day 13, we will practice using empathy to observe ourselves, looking at how our ego reacts in different environments. We will identify how our beliefs change based on our surroundings and company, and close with a ritual that helps us observe our

patterns so we can avoid getting swept away by our ego.

In metaphysics, the word *ego* describes a conscious-thinking subject. In popular culture, ego is often a person's sense of self-esteem or self-importance. In psychology, ego is the part of the mind that mediates between the conscious and the unconscious mind.

Our egos handle reality by testing and maintaining a sense of personal identity. It's the part of us that remembers, evaluates, plans, and responds to our physical world. In Sigmund Freud's description, the ego interacts with the id (the center of our primitive emotions and drivers) and the superego (the center of our morals and ethics):

Ego (Latin: "I") comprises the executive functions of personality by serving as the integrator of the outer and inner worlds as well as of the id and the superego. The ego gives continuity and consistency to behavior by providing a personal point of reference which relates the events of the past (retained in memory) with actions of the present and of the future (represented in anticipation and imagination). The ego is not coextensive with either the personality or the body, although body concepts form the core of early experiences of self. The ego, once developed, is capable of change throughout life, particularly under conditions of threat, illness, and significant changes in life circumstances.[4]

These concepts connect back to our brain and nervous system. In Phase Two, I introduced the concept of the lizard brain, a catchy term describing the amygdala. This small but powerful part of our brain and nervous system controls autonomic responses that ensure our survival: our reactions to imminent physical or emotional danger, our need to rest or to

reproduce, our need to eat to survive or even to expel what we've eaten. The lizard brain is similar to Freud's concept of id. The id reacts quickly and decisively to save our lives, but it doesn't make the most intelligent or rational choices when motivated by fear.

Both the ego and superego correspond with the largest part of our brain, the cerebral cortex. The cerebral cortex is said to be the part of our brain that sets us apart from more primitive animals. It controls how we connect and communicate, how we remember details, how we imagine, how we create. The superego governs how we interact with the world outside of us. We each have a set of moral codes that we've learned and internalized over time. Our superego helps regulate our thoughts and behavior to keep ourselves and those around us safe and in line with our shared morals. Shame is a signal to our superego to exert more control. Our superegos translate the potential for discord with the

4. The Editors of *Encyclopaedia Britannica*, "ego," *Encyclopedia Britannica*, December 15, 2021, https://www.britannica.com/topic/ego -philosophy-and-psychology.

collective to our bodies and minds in the form of shame.

The ego, however, is separate from the id and the superego and has the ability to choose. The influences and urges of our id are subtle and powerful. The weaker our self-awareness, the more likely we may find ourselves guided by our id. Our id wants us to follow the easiest path to safety and security available to us, regardless of potential long-term harm or benefits.

Our superego is perhaps less subtle, yet equally powerful. It can be difficult to distinguish between our superego (extrinsic relationships) and ego (intrinsic motivation). It requires a strengthening of self-awareness, mindfulness, and self-assessment. By using empathy to examine our beliefs, we can identify what's most resonant with our own current sensibilities, beliefs, and drivers.

I offer that we approach ego without judgment. We all have egos. Ego is who we are, how people see us, and how we see ourselves. It is our witness and our narrator. But the stories we tell ourselves aren't always the truth. Without regular self-reflection, the stories our ego tells us might become inconsistent with our values, well-being, and happiness.

There is also the view that our ego, or ability to observe, remains unchanged. In this view of the world, it is all that we observe that is constantly changing, from our understanding of our presence and existence, to our emotional responses, to the infinite universe surrounding us that we hold no control over. These are all changing, while the observer remains the same, reacting to the world around them.

It is no wonder that the question "Who am I?" has consumed the energy and imagination of so many. It is a wonderful and at times intoxicating and disorienting privilege to be able to contemplate one's self and existence.

Yet, we've practiced this awareness earlier in the book in the Language of Feelings as we checked in with our bodies and our emotions. With more comfort and skill at identifying and labeling our emotions, we were able to slow down the automatic responses driven by our id or lizard brain, gain greater conscious control over our thoughts and actions, and learn that our emotions don't define us.

I'm sure we can all recount moments where we may have acted differently because we were overly elated or in the throes of fear, anger, or sadness. These moments illustrate how our thinking self, or ego, shifts because of our emotions. When heightened emotions are at play, we run the risk of saying or doing things that do not match our intentional beliefs. In these cases, it is helpful to take a moment to let the emotion subside. Our conscious self wants us to slow down and connect with whatever part of us the emotions may be trying to protect. You now have and are continuing to strengthen this ability to slow down and connect to your self-awareness.

This ability to relax and connect supported me in reevaluating myself in the context of my relationships. The relationship I had with my parents is a prime example. I had a feeling of fear and shame, unconsciously stoked by my parents' words and actions as they attempted to protect and guide me. For most of my childhood and adult life, I had no awareness of this pattern of interaction, and no agency to say no. Whenever my parents advised me, I would flee and avoid. In the cases where I couldn't escape, I would tune out or even react in anger (another method of escaping perceived danger).

The maxims I'd been taught, such as "Honor thy mother and father" and "Don't interrupt" and "Parents know best," sat in my superego and prevented me from following my instincts to seek safety in a constructive way. My ego was affected by this dynamic. I learned to shrink in places where I perceived danger I couldn't confront with violence. This might be in situations like an application process or audition. When I was subjected to judgment or scrutiny, I would dissociate and lose some cognitive abilities. In new or large groups, I would enter with an introverted disposition. I might stay there if I never achieved a sense of safety. A belief I had was that unless I was going to be perfect, it would be better to remain unnoticed.

I learned to bully and to apply guilt to people that I trusted and loved as a way to get what I wanted. As a result, I have struggled to forge and maintain deep friendships with people who weren't responsive to these dynamics. My subconscious constructed a narrative that not responding to my subtle forms of guilt meant lack of care or loyalty. This same dynamic found itself in my failed romantic relationships. Because I was hooked on the trauma of rejection and invalidation, a pattern emerged. I would seek relationships that stoked my feelings of shame and unrequited love.

As I reflect, when I am really patient and gracious with myself, I can also identify friendship, romantic, and even family relationships that I shunned. The connections felt too secure and safe. Subconsciously, I seemed to want what wasn't best for me. My nurture taught me that punishment, cajoling, and manipulation were healthy forms of motivation to accept. As a result, I stayed way too long in jobs in which my well-being suffered. Frankly, my subconscious sense of belonging was tethered to having my self-worth challenged or attacked. Absent the ability to assess, be with, and manage my emotions, I soon found myself in a self-destructive

"Empathy gives us the ability to honor and label our emotions."

pattern of escaping, through work and from work. I escaped through partying. I escaped with romance. My behavior was completely out of alignment with my values.

Mindfulness and somatic awareness gave me the ability to make sense of my impulses and my needs. Empathy gives us the ability to honor and label our emotions, even in situations where it may not feel safe.

For much of my young adult life, I was unaware of how weak my sense of self really was. As such, I acted differently than how I felt or truly wanted to be. I acted tough at times to show people I feared that I shouldn't be messed with. I pretended to be more mature or experienced in romance and love because I was afraid to share that I was inexperienced and still learning. I couldn't recognize how my ego was working from the inside out to manifest my choices and actions. It was

simply trying to keep me feeling safe and loved.

We each have a voice in our minds that helps us reason through our steps. Are you aware of your inner voice and the quality of its beliefs and messages? Is it positive and affirming? Is it discouraging and negative? Does your inner voice vary based on the situation?

For me, the answer to each of these questions is yes! My inner voice, or ego, can be supportive, or it can send me through a labyrinth of self-sabotage. My level of fatigue, my sense of security at home and at work, and even the time of year and weather affect the quality and tone of its messages.

In Phase Two, the Importance of Intention, we developed tools for using our values and purpose to regulate and translate our emotions. Most of us can think of a time in our lives when we reluctantly went along with the popular opinion of our friends, teachers, parents, or colleagues. A time when we kept the peace to win affection or simply because we did not want to endure a challenging conversation.

These are examples of when our thinking mind willingly becomes part of a group without negotiating whether the action or opinion is right for us. In other words, when our super-ego is misaligned with our id and our ego. And too many decisions like this can cost us in the form of shame or guilt.

Shame or guilt, and the corresponding emotions and sensations that follow, are signals that we might be outside of our integrity. This might show up as tension in the shoulders, abdomen, or chest. We might feel tension, but underneath the physical sensation is an actual emotion.

Our somatic awareness helps us acknowledge the feeling of disconnection sooner rather than later. Our values and

purpose help us translate our emotional experience into a warning sign that we need to use a bit more attention and energy to manage our ego with grace.

Combined, the Language of Feelings and the Importance of Intention create a framework for witnessing our unique experiences and making more conscious and informed choices. The interaction of our emotions, extrinsic values, and intrinsic values manifests what we bring to the world around us. The Five Phases of Empathy is a suite of rituals that give us a framework for our exploration of "who we are" and what we want to bring into the world.

With the power of empathy, we understand that we are the one who observes, the one who experiences, the one who feels, and the one who reacts. However, we are not the actions, ideas, and emotions that we produce. With this foundation of freedom established, I offer that we as individuals also get to choose our beliefs. On Day 13, we begin to practice observing ourselves and noticing how our ego changes based on our environment. We are about to unlock a life-long practice of metaphysical self-assessment. You have the power to direct your beliefs and intentions from the inside outward. It is a superpower when mastered, and a savior when introduced just in time. May your path to personal growth lead you to inspire others and share this power with them.

DAY 13

Exercise

Write down your values and purpose statement.

As you prepare to explore the journaling prompts that follow, take a few deep breaths to connect to your body and your emotions. Use your imagination to travel to situations throughout your life where you are surrounded by caring people. Go to memories in which you feel safe and connected. As you visit these situations, memories, and communities, bring your purpose statement along for the journey.

Slowly and intentionally explore the journaling prompts. Apply additional attention and energy toward remaining grounded in your somatic experience and revisiting your values and purpose statement. Acknowledge and lower your ego, and be willing to learn from all the emotions—joy, fear, anger, shame, and sadness.

141

Where do you spend most of your time?

What are the values present in these spaces?

What values are you safe admitting when you are in these spaces?

What is your relationship with your family?

What values do you share with them?

What values do you have a difficult time sharing with your family?

Who are you when you are alone?

What are your values?

What values are you only safe admitting when you are alone?

Take a moment to reflect on your responses and capture what you've learned about your beliefs.

DAY 14

Vulnerable Bravery

What is one boundary you are proud to have enforced or confronted recently? What fear had to be overcome to assert yourself in that situation?

The term *boundaries*, as I've used it up to this point in the book, refers to a physical or emotional line that you or another person does not want crossed. We create boundaries so that we can be clear with the people we engage with about the actions and words that bring us discomfort. It can be hard to say no to a person you care about or whom you rely on financially or emotionally. It takes a lot of courage. Even more difficult to confront is a boundary or limitation you've placed on yourself. Conscious or subconscious boundaries are often hidden from us. On Day 14, Vulnerable Bravery, I invite you to think about your subconscious boundaries. This is a difficult topic to explore, but we will use empathy to get there together. Compassion for our internal boundaries strengthens our

ability for growth. We'll expand our self-compassion and apply it toward living an intentional, empathetic, and assertive life.

The first time someone used the term *boundaries* with me I felt shame, fear, and anger. I did not understand the word, and it almost felt as though it was being weaponized against me. My ego was triggered. My concept of boundaries wasn't even formed before it seemed I was a transgressor. My fear of having done something wrong in a space where I didn't yet feel safe made me defensive instead of being open and curious about what others were experiencing. It was a situation where I was shown a boundary that I was crossing, which ended up teaching me a lot about my own boundaries and ego-protection tendencies.

I was in my early thirties. I attended an event for wellness, social justice, and mindfulness leaders in Brooklyn, New York. I had shared a story about a trauma I'd experienced as

143

a young boy growing up in Bedford-Stuyvesant (Bed-Stuy), Brooklyn. The story contained the violence I saw on a weekly basis as a child. As I told the story, my voice elevated and took on the tense color of anger. I shared the fear I experienced through my passion and my inflection. When I finished, it was clear that my story did not leave the other participants feeling warm and fuzzy. It felt like I'd inconvenienced the group with the darkness of my reality. I saw shocked faces and distressed brows, crossed arms and adjacent whispers. Amid the clinking of utensils against plates and indecipherable verbal exchanges, my abdomen and throat clenched and my temperature rose. I left the event with a bad taste in my mouth.

I learned later from my romantic partner that I had crossed her boundaries, and several other group members' as well, when I told my story. They felt shamed by me, which they had not signed up for. I scoffed at the idea of boundaries. To me, it seemed like a roomful of people who were now living in gentrified Brooklyn neighborhoods should not be offended by the reality of the neighborhoods' past. I felt that they were ignoring their privilege and disregarding the hardship I'd experienced.

The last of four boys born to Jamaican immigrant parents, I was raised in a Bed-Stuy that was being ravaged by the crack epidemic and urban neglect. I had no choice but to orient toward survival and projected toughness. At the event that day, I thought to myself, *Y'all need to wake the hell up.*

The story I told was terrifying for many. I spoke about the gentrified neighborhoods we all were living in. I spoke of being priced out of the neighborhood where I had witnessed my older brother Darren survive gunshot trauma when I was just five years old. I spoke of my mother using her body to blockade the ambulance so that they couldn't take Darren to Woodhull Hospital. I explained that she was sure he'd die because of the reputation that hospital had. It was a hospital my hipster friends would know. Woodhull is on the border of Bed-Stuy and Bushwick, two popular neighborhoods in which a lot of the event attendees now lived. I spoke of witnessing many brutal physical fights—women fighting each other, men fighting each other, groups of people fighting each other. I took a risk sharing my background and expected empathy.

At the time, I was still afraid of being myself in these settings. I was new to wellness, community building, and community agency, and I kept finding myself in communal storytelling environments. I'd enter a room with my partner, Meghan, but we would be sorted into small groups and I'd wind up with strangers, sharing stories based on surprise prompts. Back then, I hated being put on the spot all the time. I thought

forced vulnerability sharing with strangers was invasive and disingenuous. Unknown to me at the time, I had created belief systems to protect my fear of sharing vulnerably in these groups.

So that day, after taking the risk to share, I'm not sure what I was expecting. More sympathy? Praise for having survived my past? Apologies from the group for not knowing what the locals from these parts of Brooklyn and other urban communities experiencing gentrification have gone through?

There were many judgments present in the room that day. The judgments I was most able to unpack were my own. I assumed that everyone in the group came from privileged backgrounds. I assumed that everyone in the room had more comfort with sharing than I did. I assumed people were judging me. I assumed I had grown further apart from the group, rather than more connected.

I was experiencing what shame researcher and world-renowned author Brené Brown refers to as a vulnerability hangover. A vulnerability hangover is like a drinking hangover. It feels OK or even fun while you are drinking or being vulnerable, but you regret it in the days afterward. It happens when we share something with a person or group and experience rejection, real or imagined. At that event, I thought, *Most of these people speak of being vulnerable and wear it as a badge. But when I take this risk to share my fear of vulnerability and my hardships with the group, my truth is too much for them to handle.*

Boy, was I wrong. A week later, I received a call from a gentleman name Tom. He wanted to honor me for sharing my heart-wrenching story. He shared his own story of witnessing violence as a young white boy living with a single mom outside Youngstown, Ohio. He shared the fear he feels being surrounded by people that he perceives as more wealthy, educated, and privileged than he is.

Days later at a party, a woman I didn't get a chance to meet at that gathering approached me to introduce herself. She shared that she had three brothers, like I did. She shared that they hadn't been speaking to one another much after losing both their parents. My testimony prompted her to confront her blocks around speaking with them and take a first step.

When I connected with my partner about that night, she revealed that she felt deep sympathy and care for me. She also felt pride, knowing how difficult it was for me to share my past in these settings. However, my initial reaction and defensiveness on the topic had left her feeling afraid and confused. She didn't know how to approach the topic with me, so she opted to leave the conversation alone. Because of the stories I had in my head, I'd failed to see that my partner

"Vulnerable bravery inspires vulnerable bravery."

was on my side even if what I'd shared had been hard for her to hear.

In hindsight, I learned a lot about myself and the world around me as that situation unfolded. I took a risk, and my ego was triggered. I didn't feel immediately affirmed, and I began to focus only on the potential negative outcomes. My fear of speaking and of judgment overshadowed the fact that I'd managed to take up space with my share. I had admitted a wealth gap in my upbringing. I had put my differences front and center in the room. I failed to recognize the many ways I'd exhibited and modeled vulnerable bravery in that room.

I was so committed to my internal story that I was unable to see the intrinsic values I chose to exhibit. My resilience. My passion. I failed to recognize that many were moved by my story. Yes, I had crossed a boundary for some as the violence in my story triggered fear and caused discomfort. But in this case, there were others who were grateful for being pushed outside their comfort zone. I learned vulnerable bravery can be contagious. Vulnerable bravery inspires vulnerable bravery.

Finally, I had overlooked my internal growth in overcoming an interpersonal fear. Perhaps the most important thing about that day was that I broke through a fear of sharing myself in intimate public settings. It would be a while before I'd be able to handle situations like this with ease. Gradually I learned that when I am grounded in my body, emotions, and values, vulnerability is easy. Eventually it graduates from easy and becomes a superpower.

In some ways, my body, emotions, values, and purpose are also boundaries. If I feel uneasy physically or emotionally, this might be a sign that a boundary is being crossed. If I'm aligned with my values and purpose, I can take some risks that feel uncomfortable. I know that I'm safe and have the tools to navigate myself through that uncertainty.

I also learned that day that showing one's vulnerability can be empowering, disarming, and disorienting all at the same time. I thought I'd lost connection with the group, when really, I had grabbed the group's attention and was myself too disoriented to know what to do with it.

Upon reflection, I began to see that healing was achieved through sharing my story. The things that have brought me pain and discomfort can at times be limiting beliefs that hold me back. I've come to a deeper place of understanding of the boundaries that I crossed that day. If my goal is to move people to my side and to action, then there is nothing wrong with me applying nuance to my story to ensure the emotional safety of the listeners. Now when I am

invited to tell my story, I ask as many questions as possible about my audience. I listen with all my senses even as I'm speaking, looking for clues that can add nuance to my talk. Even now, I take risks that sometimes miss the desired effect, but I still venture forward. To get to this level of grace and understanding for the people in the room means I have healed enough to think about them as much as myself.

I needed my boundary of pride and stubbornness back then as a shield. Today, I'm comfortable placing that shield to the side to achieve connection. At the time, I needed to push their potential feelings away so that I could feel affirmed in sharing my truth. Today, I know my truth has value, so I can attune to the recipients a bit more. I can suit my story to their needs and sensibilities, without feeling like I'm compromising myself or my desired outcome.

An awareness of your boundaries helps when you are

148

approaching your own internal boundary or the boundaries of another person. Everyone has boundaries, and they generally fall into three categories: rigid, porous, and healthy. A person with rigid boundaries keeps others at a distance, emotionally, physically, or otherwise. Almost a direct opposite, a person with porous boundaries tends to get too involved, or let other people get too close too soon. A person with healthy boundaries is comfortable being vulnerable, but also knows how to say no with confidence.

When we acknowledge our boundaries, we are accepting growth and change—which for so many also means confronting fear. In particular, fear of things that we cannot control. As small children, for example, with less knowledge to apply to new situations, we watch and seek guidance from our caregivers. This experience, no matter how insecure or secure, informs our own emotional responses to boundaries,

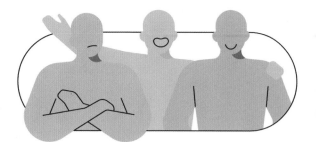

growth, and change. We absorb much from our caregivers about how to behave and what to be afraid of. In my case, my parents and my life experiences no doubt contributed to my fear of public speaking and my anxieties about my differences from others.

149

As we identify our own fears, internal and external, we can make conscious choices to hold on to them or to let them go. When we find the bravery and vulnerability to confront our limiting beliefs and narratives, we challenge how we see ourselves, other people, the world, and the future. We can face our core beliefs, good and bad, over and over again, and not only survive, but also grow through them. There is humanity and there is power in owning your vulnerabilities.

DAY 14
Exercise

1. For our Day 14 exercise, I invite you to safely explore one of your emotional blocks. Make a list of ten things you are afraid of. This might be as small as petting an animal, like a snake, or as big as setting an audacious goal for yourself, like getting a PhD.

2. Now rank your fears on a scale of one to ten, with one being the lightest ("No sweat, I got this.") to ten being the hardest ("If you think I'm even capable of bringing this to my consciousness, then you've got an inflated view of my abilities.").

3. Once you have them ranked, pick a fear that is greater than a three but no greater than a seven. Begin to imagine that fear deeply. Take a few deep breaths, and scan your body to identify where that fear resides in your body. Can you describe that fear (draw it, give it a color or sound, etc.) in a way you'll be able to understand later? Start with the physical sensations of how that fear manifests in your body. Then slowly and intentionally describe what the fear is preventing you from doing.

4. Finally, ask yourself whether you are willing to share that fear with someone close to you. The act of sharing your fear is an act of externalizing it, taking it from a mental and emotional place and bringing it into the physical world. This act also removes the fear from your ego and allows someone to support you in assessing it. As we learned on Day 13, our ego plays a powerful role in keeping us safe, but it is not always correct. Our emotions and values are one set of tools to help us make assessments on our own. They are also powerful anchors in helping us share ourselves vulnerably and accept the love and support of others.

Vulnerable bravery is a two-way street. It's about trusting our intuition and trusting those around us to survive discomfort in the name of connection, integrity, and growth. It's also an exercise in strengthening empathy. Each confrontation with fear creates new neural pathways to safety. We use empathy to assess our memories, beliefs, and biases from a new perspective. We get to reassess those ideas that no longer serve us in the ways that they once did. As we do this work individually, we become better models for how to navigate uncertainty and fear both individually and collectively. So with that, you have the tools to use vulnerable bravery to cultivate and proliferate empathy in yourself and in the people you encounter.

Your Army of Support

Who are you comfortable turning to if you find yourself in need?

For many of us, myself included, asking for help is hard. It takes vulnerability to face the potential of rejection or judgment. It takes belief that with support we can overcome our challenges. There was a time when I judged my former romantic partner for her ability to ask for help. It was a cultural difference, but also a personal one. I was afraid to ask, but she wasn't. I didn't believe that I should be told yes. What she embodied, that I eventually learned, is that we are all deserving of support. We must trust and love ourselves enough to believe we are worthy of it. For Day 15, Your Army of Support, we'll use our values and purpose to anchor in self-love. We'll use empathy for ourselves to guide us in identifying our growth and support network.

Let's face it—our capitalist society and economic structures prioritize individualism over collectivism. We compare, we rank, we aim to outdo one another. There are great benefits to separating from the pack and ending up on top in almost every aspect of our lives. From birth we measure a child's size, response rates, and family conditions as indicators of natural gifts or deficiencies. We measure against one another to predict health and intelligence. As children, standing out in class or in an activity or sport leads to more time and resources spent on that person's pursuit of excellence. As adults, being number one means more money, prestige, access, and power. Most of all, it provides a shield from the difficult emotions of not measuring up—the sadness, anger, fear, and shame of ranking below the pack.

Given the choice of individual success and collective prosperity, most people in America would find themselves hard-pressed to deny their leaning toward individual success. Many of us have been conditioned

153

to believe that we've gotten to where we are alone and that we have to continue to go it alone. But if we slow down to reflect, we begin to see that this is never true.

Take the process of birth. We need at least two people to conceive, a network of people to support our mothers through the pregnancy process, and a team of birthing and medical professionals to bring our mothers and babies through a healthy birth and recovery process.

No matter how gifted an individual may be, it takes an entire community of people to raise our children into adults. This includes family members, teachers, neighbors, friends. And as adults, we rely on people to support the infrastructure of living, from growing, harvesting, and delivering the food we eat to providing us with power, water, and waste disposal in our daily lives.

These examples focus on the practical aspects of life to show the ways both big and small that we are connected to the world around us. It's often much harder to recognize how interconnected we are with one another on an emotional level.

This lack of awareness of our emotional interconnection is often revealed and tested in moments of crisis. My own lack of awareness of the presence and power of my communal support network revealed itself to me after my relationship with my romantic partner ended and my brothers Chris and Darren died—all within three consecutive three-month periods. I began to see the gap in my emotional landscape. When I emerged from my grief, I yearned to fill the gaps that those three losses had created.

Fortunately, I did not remain there long. At this point, I had been attending my men's group meetings for nearly a year. The support I'd received from my fellow group members was unlocking new types of trust. I knew that I could turn to them via our group chat or even a one-on-one phone call to a specific man in the group when I needed support. With the group, my range of trust expanded into wider areas of vulnerability. Each of us has a willingness and base level of training to facilitate difficult emotional conversations and to protect and support those involved. The structure and consistency of this group allowed me to rewire my belief systems around the trust and intimacy that's possible to achieve in new relationships (and particularly in friendships with men).

The other key pillar that helped stabilize my emotional state was the relationship that I was forming with my now wife, Caroline. As timing would have it, we met shortly before my brother Chris died. Our initial dating had the space that I needed, since I was recently recovering from a breakup. It also had the warmth and depth of connection that I am attracted to and would come to need. Our initial courting period was short but intense. I met Caroline when she was studying in New York and writing her thesis paper for her business degree with Copenhagen Business School. She had returned to Copenhagen before my brother Chris passed away. We kept in touch and she provided support from a distance as I worked through my own inner process of discovery and healing. I remember receiving a rose quartz crystal from her in the mail. I didn't understand the meaning at the time, but I carried it as a talisman to remind me that I deserved love and healing.

"I'd use something that was free and abundant to me: my own story and my effort."

Caroline invited me to spend some time with her in Copenhagen when I desperately needed space to heal from my brothers' deaths and come to terms with the loss of my employment and the security it provided. While I was there with her, I found the nurturing support I needed to listen to my heart about what to do next.

It was one night that week that I decided to dedicate my life to spreading empathy. I'd use something that was free and abundant to me: my own story and my effort. I got the idea to go to people physically via a road trip. I'd allow my values and purpose statement to guide me. I'd use my newfound emotional awareness to confront those fears.

After the road trip, something special happened. I decided to say yes to attending an EVRYMAN retreat. The retreat offered me the opportunity to deepen my own emotional leadership skills, as well as my comfort level. It also required

overcoming another block around asking for help. Unemployed at the time, I couldn't afford the full cost of the retreat and transportation. To attend, I had to reach out and ask for a scholarship or discount on the full amount of admission.

Then, shortly after the retreat, I was back in NYC and trying to make sense of what I would do next. On this particular day, I took notice of the messages being shared on social media by a Black British gentleman who was slightly older than me. His name was Kevin Wilkinson. He was a former finance guy turned hypnotherapy, mindfulness, and fitness coach with a holistic wellness company called the Living Full Project. I really resonated with the inspirational messages he shared on Instagram.

Even though I was grateful and enjoying the relationships I was forming through EVRYMAN, I was lacking connections with men of my race. I wanted to find someone who had a deeper understanding of my experiences, past and present. I decided to reach out to Kevin to share a synopsis of my story and to ask for his help navigating grief and my issues of self-confidence and anxiety. I was afraid that I would never be able to afford his time, or that my request might be one of many that he unfortunately couldn't commit to responding to. Kevin not only responded to my message, but he also shared that he was moved by it. When we connected virtually, I learned that he also had a Caribbean background. He had also shared some of my struggles in his youth—partying, failed romantic partnerships, and a strained relationship with his father. Kevin agreed to support me in moving through my grief and to provide coaching as needed. He encouraged me to keep going with my movement to spread empathy. His belief in me provided the emotional fuel I needed to plan my next steps in the month leading up to the pandemic. Yet another stranger had entered my network of support.

I started to see and feel the power of a chosen community. I was adding a new tool to my tool belt of emotional support. As I gained a greater understanding of myself—my emotional and physical needs, and my values—the community around me transformed. What was once a source of anxiety and discomfort was becoming an amplifier of my healing, growth, and ambitions.

Around January 2020, my men's group brother Tom invited me to join him and a group of strangers in a twenty-one-day meditation challenge. It was created by Deepak Chopra and Chopra Global, his health company. I'd received invitations for communal challenges many times before, but I'd always declined. I was getting used to saying deeply intentional yeses, however, especially when I felt fear and resistance. So this time I accepted.

157

One of the hardest exercises in this challenge was one where we needed to identify our support network, the group of people who could help us achieve our purpose. On Day 15, I get to share a similar exercise with you.

I learned during the events that transpired in my life that asking for, giving, and receiving support is the cycle. This cycle fuels our light as individuals and as a species. It's reflected in our capacity for enduring hardship when we rise to the challenge together. This cycle of support is crucial to our survival and is the cornerstone of our happiness. I have compassion for the challenge of expressing vulnerability and openly giving and receiving help. This is a narrative I believe we all need support in deprogramming (and I do believe it needs to be deprogrammed). The process of unlearning individualism starts with our choices.

DAY 15

Exercise

On Day 15, I invite you to let go of fear and cultivate abundance. Reference your purpose statement and values as a reminder of what you wish to achieve, and use it as an inspiration for who can help you get there. If this is hard for you, be mindful of how fear manifests in your body. Check in on your tendencies for avoiding fear—be that procrastination, judgment of the exercise, or other forms of diversion. Are they showing up? If this is easy for you, also notice the ease you feel, and honor this privilege and super-power. Try to find a contact who represents a stretch or edge, a person who you wish to take a vulnerable risk with or is hard to reach. Reflecting on your army of support should be an active process that yields a range of relationships: people who you've overlooked or forgotten, people for whom you might harbor difficult feelings, people who embody a

159

growth hurdle, people you don't know and who would represent a leap of faith.

1. Write down the names of fifty people who have helped in your life, directly or indirectly, and who you would like to ask for help. (If fifty feels impossible, start adding people you haven't met yet but want to. Remember, you are worthy of this support system.)

2. Narrow the list to five people you will reach out to in the next week.

3. Write down one "ask" for each of the five people.

Bonus: Reach out to one person from your list to share this exercise and your request for their support with.

From Empathy to Impact

In the first three phases, we directed our focus inward. We learned how to use empathy to deepen our self-awareness and self-love. We learned rituals that increase our clarity in the face of subconscious impediments and unforeseen obstacles. We strengthened our ability to remain grounded, even when the emotions around us heighten. We audited how we interact with the world around us to find the drains on our energy. And finally, we identified the support network that helps keep us full and growing. In Phase Four we now turn our focus outward. Our ability to use empathy and emotional awareness to heal and grow now increases our capacity for compassion for others.

With greater compassion and expanded curiosity, we become better at putting ourselves in another person's shoes, from individuals, to groups, to the animals in our lives. Even for the imagined characters we dream up and actualize. Empathy and compassion make us better listeners and better storytellers.

When we gain greater comfort with our emotions, and clarity with our purpose and our boundaries, we gain a greater understanding of ego. Secure in ourselves and our emotions, we are more comfortable quieting our ego. We can surrender to the many nuanced perspectives of others and to the many new wonders we encounter.

Perspective-taking is what many people think of when they think of empathy as a concept. It is the act of perceiving a situation or understanding a concept from an alternative point of view. Perspective-taking comes naturally to some—it is typically born out of survival. The need to detect slight changes in emotions or moods could be the result of abuse, for example. Exposure to physical and emotional abuse can have a long-term effect of enhancing a person's perspective-taking ability.

161

The opposite effect can happen to those who grow up in safety and with financial or relational privileges. People who don't need to be aware of the shifts in others' moods might have a more difficult time seeing the perspectives of others around them. Their safety and access to attuned caregivers during formative years allowed them to focus their attention inward. Their need for vigilance and advanced attunement doesn't develop automatically.

Neurodivergent people, including those who have attention deficit hyperactivity disorder or autism, might also have a hard time with perspective-taking. In some cases, neuro-logical differences make it challenging to attune to the emotional cues and implicit needs of another person or to respond in a way that we typ-ically associate with empathy. This absolutely does not mean that neurodivergent people are devoid of empathy or lack the ability to hone it as a skill.

For example, a research study from 2018 has shown that some people with autism may have difficulties recognizing another person's emotional state, but not with feeling what someone else feels or desiring to respond appropriately to someone else's emotions once they've been identified.[1]

Even those who didn't develop empathy skills when they were young have the ability to expand through purposeful practice. Going from empathy to impact means taking a proactive role in protecting the safety of all in the group. Rather than shaming those who struggle to see from another's perspective, my goal is to widen our tool set, aperture, and willingness to assess how we relate to oth-ers. With greater empathy for the self and the collec-tive, we can look critically at

1. Varun Warrier, Roberto Toro, et al., "Genome-wide Analyses of Self-reported Empathy: Correlations with Autism, Schizophrenia, and Anorexia Nervosa," *Translational Psychiatry* 8, no. 35 (2018), https://doi.org/10.1038/s41398-017-0082-6.

"Going from empathy to impact means taking a proactive role."

societal power dynamics from a place of safety.

As a measure of empathy, *The Power of Empathy* follows the belief that when we are living as our full selves, our collective output is greater. This is the argument for diversity. Biological diversity. Ecological diversity. Even societal diversity, which refers to the differences seen in a particular society—diversity of religion, culture, economic status, and so forth. We all play a part, so each of our contributions is valuable.

The relationships we form with each other work in the same way. With globalization and immigration, societal contexts differ among and within nations, regions, and cities. Social diversity challenges individuals to think in new ways about their interactions

with one another. When population shifts occur and new kinds of people are introduced to society, individual groups must reassess where they stand relative to others. While social diversity can be a source of conflict, it also makes this world more livable and attractive.

163

From Empathy to Impact explores this view of the world—that each individual plays a crucial role in uplifting the happiness and well-being of the collective.

As empathetic leaders, we develop the grace and tact to navigate conflict in service of safety, well-being, and growth. By taking care of ourselves and approaching our Circles of Control and Influence with empathy, we create a ripple in every space that we touch.

Facing Your Fears

What are you afraid of, and why do you think that is?

In 2019, when I decided to head out on a four-month road trip to tell my story and share the card game Actually Curious, I was already starting to become fascinated by fear, but I didn't quite know it yet. Prior to the trip, I never felt like I had the time, resources, or freedom to embark upon an adventure such as this. The bounds of my imagination were too frequently stuck reflecting on the past or worried about the future. As I look back on that very low period of rage, doom, and confusion, I feel joy today. It was through those hardships that I learned to embody my aspirational values of grace. I tapped into core values of compassion and leadership when I needed to dig deep within myself to find relief for my sorrows, while also showing up as a source of emotional and logistical support for my family. With these anchors, alongside my childlike curiosity (which had lain dormant for some

time), I was determined to heal and grow into the value of consistency. Today I realize that in that moment, I touched fearlessness: I was no longer limited by the fears that had kept me from exploring new possibilities.

It wasn't the first time I'd thought about going on a road trip. It also wasn't the first time that I had the idea of taking Actually Curious out to the streets, where I could learn if it resonated with people. In the past I might have immediately thought, "No one wants to hear my sob story. People die all the time. What makes my story special?" Or I might have rationalized, "It's 2019; there are more efficient ways to reach people with this game."

Now, however, I remained committed. We were living through the days prior to the 2020 presidential election, with the country bitterly divided, and I believed that the Actually Curious game had the potential to help unite people. As I made my plans to travel south, a sobering note of caution from Caroline reminded me of potential dangers ahead: I would be driving long distances for the first time in my life, and I would also be driving in the southern states of America, as a Black man, alone. While I'd been thinking about this trip as a Hemingway- or Kerouac-like rite of passage, I'd forgotten the very real bias and judgment that Black people face in our country in every aspect of their lives—a bias known as far away as Scandinavia. This one reminder induced enough fear to give me pause.

When Caroline offered to travel with me, I gratefully accepted her companionship on the first leg of the trip. Her generosity with her time and energy made it possible for me to say yes to this adventure in healing and connection. I was betting on myself, my ideas, and my purpose. I recently found a powerful journal entry from this time, in which I wrote that Actually Curious "had the potential to spread tools of well-being and empathy to impact all of society for the better." Nothing was going to stand in the way of seeing if that could become a reality.

I can now revisit this road trip as a moment when I was faced with a fight, flight, or freeze choice. We don't learn that our subconscious minds might be making choices for us on subtle levels all the time through this filtering process. Our exposure to television and movies leads us to imagine dramatic situations, like a dangerous chase or a physical confrontation, when we think of fight or flight. But the reality is that we face fight, flight, or freeze situations more often than we realize. And when we subconsciously escape those situations instead of actively engaging with them, it could mean the difference between stagnation and growth.

Heading out on the trip to share Actually Curious provided me with a sense of direction. I

"I confront fear on my own terms; it's one of the keys to my happiness."

wanted to have an adventure and live out my value of curiosity, but fear had blocked the way. I wanted to heal, and as I did, my aspirational values of leadership and consistency morphed into the core value of resilience. I was determined to move past my old narratives around age and race and merit, to be seen and heard as the leader I was always meant to be. The commercial aspect of the road trip gave me a way of justifying the trip to myself and those around me. It also gave me a blue-sky dream—as silly as it seemed at the time—that a conversation game might help fight divisiveness, spread well-being, and enable opportunities for the underrepresented and underserved.

Along the way, I learned that we all face choices large and small, where our fear can prevent us from experiencing people, places, and moments that have the potential to change our lives. This could be as simple as passing up on an invitation from a new friend or mentor, or as important as missing a pivotal moment in a family member's life because the moment resurfaces negative memories from our pasts. I can tell you from experience that we are not the sum of our fears, but that our fears can teach us things we need to learn to remain safe yet willing to face limitations and challenges.

What is a fear that you are ready to overcome? Is it taking that sabbatical to write your book? Is it finally choosing to get married and start a family? Is it confronting an addiction that you've been denying? Is it asking the intriguing human at the coffee shop out on a date? Sometimes, overcoming fear can not only be a good thing, but it can also be enjoyable or even lucrative. I was somewhat forced into exploring the bounds of my fearlessness, but you have the option to do it on your own terms. Today, I confront fear on my own terms; it's one of the keys to my happiness and well-being. I hope you will let my willingness and ease at sharing difficult moments from my life inspire you to excavate the archaeological ruins of your past to unearth gems for your present and future.

Let's practice gently inviting in fear as a teacher by going inward and finding places where fear has kept us from moments of joy and wonderment.

167

DAY 16

Exercise

On Day 16, we'll practice identifying and gently examining our fears, honoring them, and being willing to learn from them. After you have answered each question, review the answers and decide what you want to take away.

Take three deep breaths and begin to check in with your somatic experience before exploring the following four questions. Pay particular attention to the emotions that might arise as you engage with each question. Where does emotion show up in your body? How does it relate to the concepts of fear and fight, flight, or freeze?

Review each question and deeply feel it in your heart, your body, and your mind. Look for an answer that presents a growth edge for you. You'll know when a clear sense of fear arises.

Once that fear is felt, thank it for keeping you safe.

Write down your answers to each question. Try to capture each fear in simple language. For example, "I am afraid to fail" or "I am afraid to face rejection."

Next, decide to let go of or keep the fear. Try using these words: "Thank you for your protective wisdom. I'm ready to release you." Or: "Thank you for your protective wisdom. I am not yet ready to let you go, and that's completely OK."

QUESTIONS:

What is one dream you've always had but never acted on? What's holding you back?

Who is one person you're avoiding? What do you need to say to or hear from this person?

What's one stereotype you've repeated because of fear that you're willing to learn more about?

Which of these fears can you confront in the next twenty-four hours?

Leading with Empathy Looks Like . . .

Think about a person, group, or community for which you would like to offer more empathy. What form of understanding and support do they need?

Leading with empathy is an exercise in humility. It requires emotional stability and awareness. It's supporting oneself, while attuning to the emotional safety of others. The ability to consistently attune to others and situations is a superpower. Empathetic leaders possess and cultivate this skill. Leading with empathy requires stacking the skills we learned over the past three phases, as well as deep knowledge of when and how to deploy them so you can intuitively do so.

Leading with empathy looks like placing the emotional quality of our interactions higher on our list of priorities than the external benefit or outcome of those interactions. When we do this in the order of processing, it requires that we attune to what we all are feeling, not thinking.

For me, leading with empathy is about dropping win-loss paradigms and control. It's not about surrendering. It's about supporting our own emotional safety. It's about being able to handle the inherent discomfort and risk associated with vulnerability and the unknown. From this place of strength and confidence, we create safety. We protect the vulnerability of others and navigate uncertainty. Emotionally secure leaders produce unexpected yet intentional solutions to unique challenges.

Leading with empathy can sometimes lead to decisions that don't make sense to others. In March 2020, most of us had no idea that the way our entire planet lives and interacts was about to be disrupted. I remember being in New Orleans around the ninth of March. I was several days into a cross-country drive that had originated in Salinas, California. I had visited my nieces and nephews to celebrate my brother Darren's

170

heavenly birthday. I needed to support my niece, who'd been recently hospitalized after an accident. It was an emotionally charged visit.

My nieces and nephews, along with my brother's widow, were navigating the distribution of Darren's estate in the absence of a will. My mother had hoped I'd act as an influential adviser. For various reasons, I ended up keeping my distance from the financial and emotional entanglement of it all. There wasn't much I could do to help.

In New Orleans, I remember sitting in my car, killing time before joining up with a crew. I had met them at a shop where I'd hosted an event for Actually Curious. It was wonderful— eight people gathered in a colorfully decorated loft on Magazine Street, baring our souls, expanding our willingness and ability to connect. It was my last group event in real life. That night was to be one last goodbye before the pandemic landed.

As I bided my time, a call came in from my lawyer and mentor, Earl, referencing a cryptic email from my ex–business partner's lawyer. My ex–business partner had removed money from the Actually Curious business account, money I'd earned driving door to door selling the game. She did this to create leverage in our separation negotiations. I was devastated, angry, and afraid.

I was running out of money as it was. But worst of all, a person whom I once considered my best friend had moved so far from our shared past that she would do something to intentionally hurt me. That realization broke my heart. Our once loving relationship was beyond repair. Instead of going out to meet this gang of young New Orleanians, I returned to my Airbnb to release the sadness and anger that arose, regroup, and plan my steps home. I then canceled a few planned events and decided to nix making my way to the densely populated New York

"Born from resilience and empathy, I find the grace to lead with consistency."

City. Instead, I made a quick stop in Tallahassee and met up with two friends from previous drives, a shop owner named Kathryn and a vintage fashion entrepreneur named Matt. Matt brought his friend Lamont, a recent PhD recipient and future university professor, who has also become my friend and a supporter of our movement to spread empathy.

On March 13, the day the lockdown began in the United States, I made my way home to my parents in Florida. I remember my feeling of confusion. The reality of my impending stagnation crept in. I did not know when I'd ever leave my parents' house. I began to experience my parents' fear of contracting the virus. They are both high-risk individuals due to their age and health history, which meant my every move would be even more scrutinized than it would have been before.

I remember taking on two opportunities to pitch for free-lance strategy work. I worked several days on both, only to have the potential clients ghost without even a response to my work. The anger, sadness, and fear grew. I remember watching on TV as the virus spread throughout the world. It was particularly raging in Italy; I watched videos of people singing to one another from balconies.

I redid my values and purpose that day. I arrived at the statement "Born from resilience and empathy, I find the grace to lead with consistency."

The next day, at my daily 4 a.m. check-in call with Caroline, we came up with the idea to make a free PDF of the Actually Curious card game. People were socially distanced and struggling with connection. We drew on our values and asked our community for help translating the free PDF into different languages. By the next day, we had seven translations. And by the following day, we could see it had been downloaded thousands of times.

It was truly remarkable for the two of us to see our idea manifest with such ease and to such a positive reception and outpouring of support. We were entering the fabric and ecosystem of our species' willingness to support, love, and provide. A miraculous thing happened as we were giving the game away—our sales also started to multiply.

All my life, and especially when I was worried about the judgment of my parents, I made decisions based on money and safety. But for the past five months, I had been making radical choices and decisions that felt good and supported my healing. For five months, I chose to let go and return to my values, letting my emotional awareness guide me. I chose to believe in me, though there was a tired and beaten voice in me wondering if I'd ever catch a break. I'm glad that I stuck to it. We were starting to see the light at the end of the tunnel. Our big break was only days away.

My past had taught me to grasp at plans and expectations, and to stress and protest when my visions fell through. So I let go of the past stories and the rigid expectations. I allowed empathy to guide me, leaned into my newly enhanced physical and emotional awareness, values and purpose, integrity, and patience. Things changed when I felt safe and full enough to offer generosity even as I struggled. The benefits might have taken a bit longer to start flowing my way, but the abundance and sense of ease hasn't left since.

173

DAY 17

Exercise

For Day 17, begin to cultivate this gift of empathetic leadership in yourself. I invite you to connect to your own inner voice. Listen for guidance, empowerment, inspiration, and intention. Take three deep inhales and three slow exhales. Scan your body for emotional sensations as signals to investigate with slow intention. When you feel present in your body, make note of your somatic experience as you journal your responses to the following prompts.

Where do you hold power?

Who do you want to share your power with?

What is your intention for sharing your gifts?

Modeling Safety and Support

In what spaces do you struggle to bring your full self? Among certain friends? In particular circles at work? Perhaps around some family members?

Some of you might be lucky enough to feel free to be your full self in all situations. If that is you, then I challenge you to imagine a situation where you might not feel safe. Perhaps in a situation where you are the "only" in some way? When we find discomfort in our lives, we are also opening the door to empathy. We work on our own emotional awareness so that we can cultivate grace and compassion—qualities that help us remain grounded in the presence of heightened emotions. The ability to remain grounded requires psychological safety, which is not a skill set everyone is capable of using. Our nature, nurture, and past experiences give some of us a higher baseline of patience, grace, and sense of safety than others. Regardless of how you answered the reflective questions at the start of this

section, the more attention and intention you bring to your emotional reactions, the more safe, confident, and impactful you will feel. This process is amplified by leading with empathy and protecting vulnerability in groups. Today, we'll start to examine our role in the various communities we inhabit. Together, we begin to set intentions for the impact we wish to deliver in the spaces that matter to us most.

175

Many arguments and negotiations fail before they begin. The parties overlook creating a sense of safety. Uncomfortable conversations trigger emotions of fear, shame, sadness, and even anger. Our inner work to remain grounded through our own emotions is significant because the conversations we face today around diversity, polarization, COVID-19, and other issues are deeply uncomfortable.

Many of us know this to be true. But few of us practice observing how our own cognitive abilities change in tense situations, let alone how group dynamics change when heightened emotions are introduced.

When a group or community is threatened, the least fortunate of the group has the hardest time being heard. As a result, they also bear the most significant burdens of unexpected change. Leading with empathy means we are vigilant for situations in which voices and opinions end up marginalized.

Many of us have likely encountered the term *safe space* in our homes and workplaces as discussion around racial justice and bias-motivated violence increased. Safe spaces are places that are free of bias, conflict, criticism, or threatening actions, ideas, or conversations. In the United States, the term originated out of the LGBTQIA+ community. It now extends to places that center other marginalized voices. Safe spaces gather empathetic leaders to explore shared experiences and purpose.

Safe space was a term that would become central to my narrative beginning around 2018, although it wouldn't become a regular part of my vocabulary until a few years later.

We created Actually Curious in 2018 to be a tool that helps groups build safety gradually as they progress through a game session. I knew from my own experience that even with a game to facilitate safety, many of us (myself included) struggle to find our voice in groups. This intensifies when the conversation shifts to important topics that have the potential to elicit polarized responses. I had a fear of being judged for sharing a response that wasn't informed enough, opinionated enough, smart enough. I struggled to find my own inner love and knowledge so I would feel safe allowing my voice to be heard.

Today, I continue to have difficulty encountering challenges and navigating interpersonal conflict. At times, confronting a client or even a past colleague took so much preparation that I'd require days after the confrontation to rest. These rituals of preparation and recharging for social situations were new to me. I didn't know it then, but my years of working hard and playing hard to cope with my life had led to undiagnosed burnout. My nervous system had been agitated for so long that I now had difficulty regulating myself normally. I lacked trust in myself when it came to being social and subjected to judgment. The adversity I experienced forced me to adopt skills in empathy to maintain resilience and to make measured decisions along the way. Gradually, I would test my fears of speaking up in groups and speaking up for myself.

In 2019, I found myself in one unexpected conflict after another. A former client was attempting to use legal force to keep our company from compensation we were entitled to. The client was someone I had considered a friend, which made things even more difficult for me. And that conflict was exacerbated by the difference in opinion on how to deal with it between me and my then girlfriend and business partner. It was the last straw in our rocky business and romantic entanglement, which meant I lost two important relationships to this conflict.

On top of it all, I was running out of money and stalling my landlord on rent while searching for free or low-cost places to stay. I rented out my apartment on Airbnb to cover my expenses. My sense of home was severely disrupted. I was also worried my family would find out and pile on the shame. I hid from their calls and visits. Just as I found a job that might help me balance it all, my brother Chris died.

This period greeted me with a heavy dose of change and conflict. I was trying to show up as a CEO of Curiosity Lab, and then as a chief marketing

"Our lives do not exist neatly in the individual spaces we inhabit."

officer and leader of a team of ten people. Behind the scenes, I was feeling very insecure and unsafe. My psychological safety was severely compromised. But it was when my brother Darren died in 2019 and I was immediately fired from my job that I became emotionally unstable.

The term *psychological safety* is most associated with the shared belief that the team at work is safe for interpersonal risk-taking. It's the ability to show and be yourself without fear of negative consequences to your self-image, status, or career. The factors that affect our financial security permeate all parts of our lives. After over two years of living through the COVID-19 pandemic, a truth that always existed became magnified. Our sense of safety at home and out in the world affects our sense of safety at work, and vice versa. Our lives do not exist neatly in the individual spaces we inhabit with no practical or emotional overlap.

My lack of psychological safety during the time of my brothers' passing forced me to identify how the fears or needs of others might cause them to act in ways that were painful to me. I eventually learned to find safety by going inward, through listening to my body and applying my values. Through the hardship, I learned how to use empathy to create a safe space for myself internally. In turn, I began to receive signals about the world around me through my emotional reactions.

Although the changes and questions still brought me fear, the values I'd established that summer helped me remain grounded and gave a map back to safety. My values of strength, resilience, leadership, consistency, and curiosity helped me think about responding to my situations proactively. I used the language of feelings to slow down and accept reality. I used my values to slowly decide my next steps.

Those days, I would often find myself overwhelmed with sadness, anger, fear, and shame. The world around me was moving so fast. The one thought that kept me centered was wanting to model strength and resilience for my nieces and nephews. They had been left without a father, and I wanted them to know that they had the will to not only survive this but also to carve out a different life for themselves. I wanted to let my individual struggles model a hero's journey, showing my loved ones what's possible.

As one of my values, curiosity had at times been a source of both inspiration and shame. I wrestled with the adventures and diversions curiosity had led me to pursue in the past. I felt shame for the immature choices of my youth. I choose to look upon that core part of myself with compassion, patiently feeling the pain and tension in my heart, my throat, and my gut.

The support I needed from myself in that moment was acceptance of my past and belief that I was a good person. I embraced my curiosity with love, and during this time, my curiosity led my healing. I chose to use my healing to bring my and my family's story to the world through another adventure: that first big road trip.

I'd decided that my brothers, two hardworking Black men chasing the American dream, dying before the age of fifty due to heart conditions, was a story that needed to be told. For me it meant that perhaps I, and people generally, deserved more longevity. My family, our larger community of Black people, marginalized people, all people. My brother's death and the pain we suffered would not be for nothing. I'd give it all meaning by sharing what I was learning with the world.

For me, at that moment, I decided I'd never again have my safety and my worth depend on an employer.

179

I decided to follow my heart, my soul, and my values where they led me. I trusted that my values of consistency and integrity would help me bring this message and tools for healing more broadly to the world. I was ready to surrender to empathy and let the cage of fear and scarcity that I lived in gradually fall away.

It was on the Actually Curious road trip that I leaned into my values and found the strength to challenge my inner fears and beliefs. Instead of remaining in my anxious and reclusive bubble, I closed my eyes and plotted my route into the lives of old friends, old adversaries, and hardest of all, into the lives and consciousnesses of strangers. I found the strength to believe that my existence mattered.

I saw that those losses in my life, at that moment, all had meaning. As I shared this purpose with people I reached out to and met, I learned to appreciate both the yeses and the nos to my requests for their time. Through the bravery to face rejection, I was affirming myself. The invitations into homes, the time granted to me to speak or demo Actually Curious, and the yeses from others affirmed me even more. I was following my inner voice. I was gaining compassion for the risky side of my curiosity. I was healing my wounds and laying new neural pathways. I was sharing myself with the world, and it proved to be more beneficial to my healing than I'd initially imagined.

The most healing and affirming part of it all was the effect my story had on people. I found myself meeting people who had experienced grief. My sharing gave them safety and permission to share their grief with me, too. In some cases, people were articulating their pain for the first time ever with me, a stranger.

In my family, I watched as the reception to my work went from concern, to judgment, to acceptance, to pride. Eventually

"Grace for ourselves and compassion for those we care about are essential."

I saw family find their own path to self-awareness, healing, and growth. As I modeled emotional awareness, intentional response, and firm boundaries, my way of being shifted their reactions from resistance to mirroring.

Soon, my story was resonating with the media and mass audiences. I invested my first earnings in securing a publicity partner to amplify my story. We agreed that my message was helpful to individuals who were trying to negotiate their own challenging emotions. We were able to combine our shared superpowers to amplify tools of empathy. Somehow this introvert with social anxiety was beginning to inspire change and action. I was taking care of me, saying yes when it mattered, and saying no when I felt genuinely unsafe or overextended. Today, I can admit it

is easier, but far from easy. As I turn toward my values and well-being, the world unfolds around me in a way that is complementary to my purpose and sense of happiness.

Leading with empathy is endless and often thankless. The benefit is that we gain the ability to support our own safety and the capacity to advocate for our values and view of the world. We will need that capacity, especially when we fall short or life suddenly spirals out of control.

Empathy allows for grace for ourselves and compassion for those we care about during difficult times. It's an essential tool if we want to show up, day in and day out, sharing our support.

DAY 18

Exercise

For Day 18, I invite you to list five circles or communities that you are involved in. This could be your family, your job, a sports team or hobby group, a community group you volunteer for, or even a community from which you've been absent.

With this list, revisit your purpose statement. Through the lens of your values, answer these questions for each circle:

1. First, "Who am I in this circle when I bring my full self?"

2. Now turn your lens outward and ask yourself, "Who in this circle might be having a difficult time bringing their full selves? And why do I feel this might be?"

3. Finally, ask yourself, "What is one thing I can do to help make every present moment in this circle more connecting, fulfilling, and impactful for myself and everyone else involved?"

The act of sharing and receiving support is a crucial cycle of life. Use this exercise to expand your safety and impact in the spaces that matter most to you.

Privilege and Bias

What are three privileges you are grateful for?

I invite you to gently embrace all the emotions that come up when you think about this question. Welcome this question as part of your gratitude practice.

Our privileges can be a source of shame in our society when they needn't be. By Day 19, we are equipped with the tools to explore how our privileges can create and protect our biases. By honoring our privileges with vulnerability, we become more aware of the things that bring us happiness and abundance. Gratitude gives us the emotional capacity to cultivate humility. The more full and happy we feel, the more capacity we have for considering the challenges others face.

A privilege can be defined as a special right, advantage, or immunity available to a person or group. It might also be defined as a special honor. These definitions aren't in themselves problematic. Yet there

are very strong feelings around the word *privilege*.

In modern parlance, *privilege* has come to mean an advantage that is undeserved. It typically refers to the access, safety, and security afforded to the wealthy and powerful in the United States and around the world. Those wealth and power dynamics also disproportionately advantage people who identify as white.

Discussion of race, wealth, and power is important because the national debate around these topics is so polarized. This stark division has given rise to protests and even acts of mass violence. In May 2022, the country watched as news unfolded of a young white man who had entered a Buffalo, New York, supermarket and murdered ten Black people. He referenced rhetoric and fear about white people being replaced by people of color. His heinous act was motivated by fear of losing his privilege. This man killed people to protect the advantages he felt were owed to white people like him.

It is difficult to engage with any topic that questions one's merit without triggering emotions of fear, anger, and shame, particularly in a world where we are so deficit- or scarcity-oriented. Empathy, in the form that I've chosen to practice, requires that I arrive at some understanding for the thought process that leads to such a heinous act. The best I can come up with is this: Something about that man's conditioning led him to believe he's in competition with others.

From birth, we are constantly pitted against one another. The language we use to describe our resources, our objects, and our blessings seems to always come imbued with scarcity. With small shifts in language, we can begin to see an abundant view that is possible. Let's consider how we commonly define privilege. According to the Merriam-Webster online dictionary, "privilege is a right

or immunity granted as a particular benefit, advantage, or favor." What if the definition went something like this: "Privilege is a special right, advantage, or immunity granted or available to any person who intentionally seeks it"? How does that change make you feel? Where do you feel it? Do you still want it as much?

The first time I explored this question, I noticed a pain in my abdomen and confusion in my mind. I was alongside a group of fifty thought leaders. We wrote the questions on privilege included in the Actually Curious: Human Rights edition, a version of the game designed to push our individual and group growth around human rights topics. When I contemplated the question on a rational level, I wanted to share my privileges. However, on an emotional level, I needed to reconcile some physical sensations of loss—the same feeling I'd had in my chest when my heart felt broken over a ruptured relationship and a similar feeling in my gut to that feeling of shame and challenged self-worth.

I took a breath, and I worked to be honest with myself and slowly connect to my body to assess the dissonance between my intentions and my somatic awareness. For privileges to become abundantly available, the idea of special privileges has to be taken away. Unfortunately, we have not been prepared to accept that loss. I, too, am biased toward wanting small advantages and privileges over others. My body knows that, whether I'm willing to admit it or not.

Soon, you'll get to explore your privileges with love and vulnerability. But before you do, I invite you to look at the bigger picture. When we talk about human rights, what are the topics and issues that matter to us all? What are you willing to fight for? Where do you stand?

Since the beginning of the COVID-19 pandemic, we have watched as moral and cultural shifts unfolded rapidly. It has become easier to imagine seismic changes in values than it may have been in the past, and to see what that would look like.

Not too long ago, the debate over abortion rights in America appeared to be a thing of the past. As I write this book, abortion laws have been rolled back on a state-by-state level, thanks to a ruling by the highest court of our nation.

LGBTQIA+ rights, hard-fought for since the '60s and beyond, also face opposition. A wave of legislation in states like Texas and Florida threatens the safety of millions. We've witnessed national and interpersonal shifts in perception around gender and sexual freedom. Has the fear of living in safety because of your gender or preferences ever caused you danger or held you back? This is a relatable place to examine the ways large and small that our privileges might exist and mask unconscious biases.

Through thoughtful and secure journaling, I was able to unearth my privileges and the biases they obscured. Two easy and obvious ones are that I am a heterosexual man. In most cases, I don't live in fear of judgment for my sexuality or gender. I was able to reflect with compassion on the challenges and threats faced by women and the LGBTQIA+ community. I was able to feel the shame and sadness that arose when I recalled that I, too, have acted in ways that were harmful to others who do not possess the privileges I hold. Even as I admit this truth, I can feel my throat clench and my arms freezing. My privileges and the biases that have been a part of my life as a result have produced challenging physical and emotional reactions.

I'm not proud that I acted outside of my integrity in the past. I'm proud that I'm aware of how my ego—my fear, shame, sadness, anger, and pursuit of joy—acted out in ways I will never repeat. I can endure the challenging emotions to truly see and accept my mistakes. I can make the conscious choice to recognize, understand, accept, and change how I behave going forward.

We've been primed with years of fear-baiting and a rise of violence in our nation. The prolonged COVID-19 lockdown and the rise in inflation has coincided with an increase in gun-related incidents and gun purchases. Where do you stand on the topic of gun ownership? Is it a privilege that matters to you? Or one you would gladly give up?

We have to have these conversations in our multicultural, multi-gendered, multi-ability schools, hospitals, workplaces, and institutions. We must have some understanding of the perspectives, emotions, and situations confronted by our peers and constituents to effectively advocate for their

187

safety. To be able to stand in these conversations, we need to rebuild ourselves from the inside out, as we have been working toward over these last few weeks.

We can use our newly cultivated abilities in empathy to place ourselves in one another's shoes. Our imaginations can transport us backward and forward to different points of time in our own lives and help us step into the experiences of others. Our time spent in the past allows us to redo, reconcile, relive, heal. And when we approach the future with kindness and love, it yields ideas, plans, creations, manifestations, and miracles.

Perspective-taking really is a human gift that can be used to unlock greater understanding and abundance. We can imagine what it feels like to be without a privilege. But I caution you: When perspective-taking intermixes with personal

and social trauma, we can find ourselves mired in comparison, projection, hatred, and obsession. We can disconnect from the humanity of another when feelings of fear, shame, anger, or sadness rise to the surface. This happens, and the "other" becomes a threat. We find ourselves lost in ego, and bias prevails.

Our perspective on an idea or a thing—mine, yours, ours, theirs—these are choices. Our goal is to strengthen our individual ability to decide. We can decide to choose curiosity instead of competition and bias.

DAY 19

Exercise

For Day 19, I'll guide you through an exercise to practice exploring your privileges in a safe space. You'll identify areas for inquiry and growth. You will devise a plan for how your curiosity, action, and intentional learning will yield expansiveness in your life and the lives of loved ones.

What privileges are important to your happiness?

> How does it feel when you focus on each privilege?
>
> Where in your body does that show up?
>
> What emotions do you associate with that physical feeling?

What privileges do you have that your family or romantic partner does not have?

> How does it feel when you focus on each privilege?
>
> Where in your body does that show up?
>
> What emotions do you associate with that physical feeling?

What privileges do you share with the majority of your coworkers? Which don't you share?

> How does it feel when you focus on each privilege?

> Where in your body does that show up?

> What emotions do you associate with that physical feeling?

What privileges do you have that people in your community do not share?

> How does it feel when you focus on each privilege?

> Where in your body does that show up?

> What emotions do you associate with that physical feeling?

What privileges do you wish to share with all of society?

> How does it feel when you focus on each privilege?

> Where in your body does that show up?

> What emotions do you associate with that physical feeling?

Third Body Exercise

Have you ever had the responsibility of making a decision on behalf of a group?

If you are a parent, you do this often. If you are part of a team at work or at school, you do this to stay organized. Based on your personality and experience, you may jump forward or slip to the back during these situations. There is no right or wrong way to show up, but it's good practice to notice and become aware of your patterns. The question we will explore on Day 20 is, "When making decisions for the group, how do you ensure that all the people you represent are considered?"

Over the past nineteen days we've used empathy, as well as contextual and social awareness, to explore the world. We've practiced tools that help us approach life with the intention of creating greater safety, inclusivity, and impact.

Today, we explore what bringing our tools of empathy together in a group setting

might look and feel like. We will do this through an activity called the Third Body Exercise. It uses somatic awareness, values and purpose, and radical curiosity and compassion to strengthen group perspective-taking.

I was first exposed to the Third Body Exercise through my EVRYMAN men's group. The group consists of seven men who commit to meeting with one another every week. If someone needs to miss a group meeting, we foster accountability by sharing with the group any needs that take priority over attendance. The group has bylaws that articulate our unified values and intentions as well as the rituals that support the group's safety and growth.

One of the weekly rituals is the opening check-in and checkout format. The check-in and checkout is like the somatic awareness self-check-in skills that we learned in Phases One and Two. After a meditation, which slows us down and

191

gets us grounded in our bodies, we each share a quick body scan of our physical condition and then a high-level emotional audit identifying feelings of joy, fear, anger, shame, or sadness. After we check in and before each individual gives their seven- to ten-minute share for the week, we do a "third body check-in." Each member has the opportunity to speak on behalf of the collective.

This weekly ritual has us checking in on the health of the group. We address questions like "Does this meeting time still work for us all?" or grievances like "Have several people been missing group more often? Does this need discussion?"

Sometimes the Third Body Exercise is heartwarming. Other times it can be confrontational and challenging. However, it is among the elements that has contributed most to the deepening of group trust and connection. In this transparent, engaged, and highly accountable atmosphere, everyone

does their best to attune to the group. It creates the conditions for total group presence no matter the outcome of the actual reactions to the prompts presented. When the group is in harmony or alignment with the person speaking on behalf of the collective, we witness the group sharing in the emotions being expressed under the words. When a few or many don't feel included in the sentiments expressed, the group experiences emotional dissonance in a pronounced way. Otherwise, outside of the group exercise setting these feelings may never come to the surface.

The Third Body Exercise can feel awkward at first because the act of speaking on behalf of the collective is awkward. Yet we do it all the time without practice or intention. I began to realize that the act of taking the perspective of the group is applicable in all interpersonal situations. From engaging with siblings, to romantic relationships, to professional or philanthropic groups, the more accurately we attune to the groups we are part of, the better we are at being a proactive player in resolving conflicts and challenges. Perspective-taking makes us better at incorporating the members in that group.

DAY 20

Exercise:
The Third Body

Many of us would agree that a group of people is almost always smarter than any one person. Yet few of us actively practice the skills required to maximize all the talents of the groups we inhabit.

Think about the early stages of any new group activity or exercise. Typically, we have empathetic teachers, coaches, mentors, and guides who help get us started. Unless someone steps up to create a sense of alignment in the group, the conscious or unconscious group dynamics begin to unfold. This is where less assertive voices get left out. This is one way that dynamics of power, privilege, ambivalence, and ignorance are perpetuated.

The Third Body Exercise is a way to stretch our ability to create safety in groups. It helps us practice taking a step back to watch group thinking in intricate detail. In this exercise, we practice the frequent and uncomfortable task of speaking on behalf of the collective. This is one of the few exercises in this book that requires the recruitment of partners.

1. Create a group (two to seven people), either virtually or in person. Try to make the group as diverse as you are able without significant effort.

2. Once your group is gathered, you will share the provided prompts. However, instead of answering from your own perspective, each person imagines speaking for the collective.

3. To help your group get the most out of the exercise, it may be helpful to share a few words about the work you've been doing to increase your capacity and abilities in using your natural tools of empathy.

4. To help people relax and increase the awareness of their somatic experience, lead the group in a short individual check-in. Invite everyone to take three deep inhales followed by long exhales. Then share a brief body scan ("Physically I'm feeling . . .") and emotional check-in ("Emotionally I'm feeling . . ."). Close your check-in and allow the next person to start their check-in by saying, "I'm here and I'm checked in."

This exercise is about embodying the perspective of the collective. You can perform this exercise with two or more people.

Read the following script:

> In any community engagement, there is me (my body), there is you (your body), and there is us (the third body).
>
> This exercise asks that we speak on behalf of the third body by answering each question from the perspective of the collective. Do this by beginning each statement with "On behalf of the third body . . ." and ending with a position that articulates a shared experience or belief rather than an individual one.
>
> An example of this might be "On behalf of the third body, I believe that we are excited and nervous about this exercise because we've never done it before."
>
> Remember, instead of answering from your own perspective, imagine yourself as speaking for the collective: "On behalf of the third body, I believe we . . ."

QUESTIONS TO EXPLORE:

What moral or cultural values do you hold in high regard and why?

How do you love?

Is higher education a right or privilege?

Is there anything too serious to be joked about?

What does it mean to lead a life well lived?

One of the dominant conflicts of our collective pasts is that many of us grow up believing that we do not have enough. Not enough money or possessions. Not enough love and friends. Not enough accomplishments and appreciation. It would seem the more we have, somehow the more we need. My favorite rapper as a kid popularized the phrase "mo' money, mo' problems." I grew up in the same impoverished neighborhood that he did, and I knew that meant that as wealth increased, so too would negative attention and energy. People would emerge who envy, take issue, or simply are conspiring to take money from you. Narratives like this one have informed my perception of wealth. My subconscious belief was that money always involves struggle. As I experienced loss, my relational, material, and emotional world got reduced to my rock bottom. My concepts of wealth, abundance, and happiness began to shift. No amount of money or material possessions,

at that moment, could buy back my happiness. I had to rebuild from an infinite internal emotional and spiritual place. I used the empathy skills I'm sharing with you in this book to find that place. The gradual exploration and renewal left a more connected and abundant me saying, "STOP spreading these false scarcity narratives about living."

Phase Five, Living with Abundance, is about our view of the world. It's about identifying and redirecting scarcity-creating narratives in our lives to recognize and magnify the abundance that's present in our world.

When we take our first breath in the morning, it means we've awakened from our sleep and have another day to live. We can let that be our first moment of gratitude, if we choose to do so. Making a ritual of waking with gratitude for another day and another breath has the power to illuminate the small pleasures in our present lives.

199

Abundance! From this place of awakened gratitude, it's nourishing to reflect and collect our ideas. What would it look like to have our dreams and awareness turn toward what we have and cherish, rather than what we don't have and what we desire?

Have you ever noticed a group of children competing for attention with one another? Perhaps at a playground or a classroom? Most of them jostle for the teacher's attention, while a few are not competing at all. Rather, they are working and playing independently. Engaging with one another at times. Watching. Resting. Each child plays out behavior indicative of their personality type and needs. Each receives the sort of attention that they bid for, right? If, for example, one child falls and begins to cry, that social ecosystem will adjust to give the child the additional attention they need. The abundance of attention and love! A classroom with small children can be a wonderful example of abundance because we can all relate to the innocence we once possessed. To a child, the world is new and wonderful. This is, sadly, until their worldview is changed through interacting with adults.

A well-attuned caregiver will notice needs beneath the surface of the behavior. A child's bids for attention in the classroom might reflect an extroverted child. It might also reflect a child who is starved for focused attention at home. The child who is quiet and reserved might naturally enjoy independence. However, we must also be vigilant for withdrawn children, as that behavior may be indicative of stress, instability, or even abuse in the child's home. Are some children happier than others? How much more attention does one child need over another? What is the best way to provide that additional attention, and at what cost? Who is to judge their individual happiness? A parent or a caring teacher may instinctively take notice and create

"Joy is abundant if you know where to look."

an environment of safety that invites that child to share. Their love for that child and that calling in life to support children helps them tap into their natural inner knowledge to navigate the situation. They find the best way to communicate with that child while tending to all the children's needs. The children are able to receive the abundance of instinctual knowledge and love!

That same instinctual intelligence can be applied to ourselves and to the people and situations we encounter. The Five Phases of Empathy shows us how to connect to our own emotions, purpose, fears, and ambitions while honoring that pursuit in others. We have learned to have compassion for the universal pursuit of safety and happiness. We've explored the idea that our scarcity is often more imagined than actual, regardless of how much we have. Today we practice deprogramming the belief of scarcity and committing to the opposite. No person

or thing can take away our joy and abundance!

When we are paying attention, our joy can spring from the simplest things. Our first breath or sound or movement or feeling of the day can be a wellspring of joy. Even understanding a difficult emotion, enduring the wave, and surviving it to experience again can be a wellspring of joy. I love arriving at a playful smile after realizing my power to release a fit of fear or anger. You, too, can feel joy simply by noticing your emotions and observing, amplifying, learning, and letting go. Joy is abundant if you know where to look, and the power of empathy teaches us how and where to look.

You see, with so much abundance available to us, we are not in competition with one another. The things that matter most—the experiences and knowledge that we collect, the time spent with the people we love, the ideas we get to express, the people

201

we get to help with our presence on the earth—they are abundant and omnipresent when we know how and where to look. We don't need to compete for those things. It is only when we believe that what we need is scarce that the world becomes competitive. We compete for land, resources, and money. What might it look like for our communities if nothing stood in the way of abundance? What would happen if we propagated the free sharing of knowledge and resources to the places in need, without restrictions like language barriers and borders? What would our schools look like? What would our neighborhoods look like? What would our medical infrastructures and facilities look like? What are the limits of our imagination and capabilities? Rather than feed into the narrative of scarcity, what if we only lived in a potentiality of abundance?

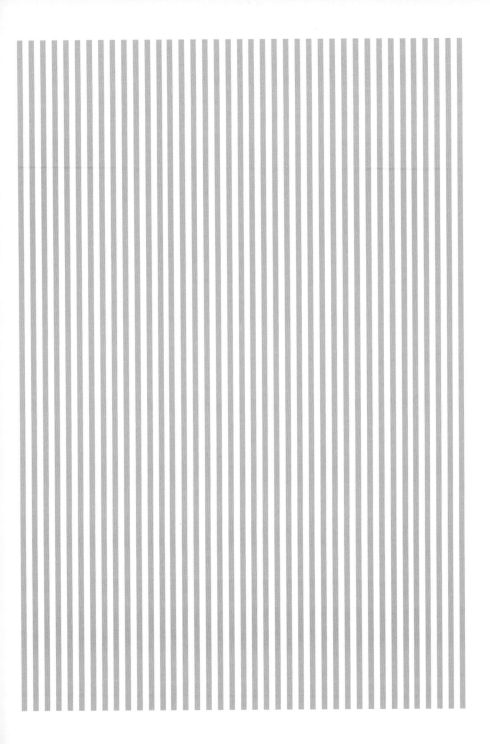

What is missing in your life? Is there anything you would like more of?

Don't be shy about it. The first step to receiving your desires is to state them. But the problem is that too few of us are told this. Instead, we are trained to believe the opposite—that what we need or desire requires struggle. This is a scarcity mindset. It's when you are so consumed with what you lack that it distracts you from living your purpose. Under a scarcity mindset, life is a finite pie, and if one person takes a big piece, that leaves less for everyone else. Scarcity is born out of fear—the fear of failure or rejection or judgment for what you don't have—and as we've learned together, our minds and hearts cannot be in a place of fear and a place of love at the same time. So, from a place of love for ourselves, Day 21 is a guide to honoring the fear that feeds our scarcity mindset.

As an adult who grew up surrounded by poverty and raised by parents who had survived even worse poverty, I know that the feeling of scarcity is a serious matter. The myth of scarcity is hardwired in me and in many of us to protect us from what our ancestors had to endure. A parent who has endured financial hardship might prioritize teaching a strong work ethic, frugality, and cautious skepticism. It is a part of the resilience I was taught, and I can attest that it is difficult to unlearn. And worse, when I've been down, it would sometimes appear that the world was conspiring to keep me in a place of need. When I was broke and behind on my bills, every unexpected call or email contained a new challenge for me to juggle. This too is a learned narrative that I had to let go. It may have felt true for a time. Now that time has passed, I can see both how short that period was and my own role in creating it with my actions or inaction. I couldn't see that then.

People who are struggling to feed their families, find access to adequate health care, and secure a safe shelter where they can lay their heads at night know that the momentum of scarcity is hard to break, especially when you are in the depths of it. Attempting to convince them that scarcity is not real might bring about feelings of fear, shame, sadness, and anger. It's important to honor the real experiences of individuals in need. My goal isn't to deny the existence of scarcity, but rather to examine the power the concept of scarcity has in our lives. I want you to see the places where your thoughts, beliefs, and emotions might allow you to reduce the stranglehold of scarcity on your own life.

Today, I am privileged to have achieved a life where my basic needs are taken care of, and I can begin to accumulate wealth. I have all my debt paid off, aside from a mortgage. I am not a millionaire (yet). Although I have savings, I don't yet have such an abundance of resources that there's no possibility of losing it all and then needing help. Yet, I feel more abundant than I ever did because I've come to learn that my happiness is not anchored to my needs and possessions, but rather to how I feel about the way and with whom I spend my time. Through the tragedy of loss and by the power of empathy, I zeroed in on my happiness code. I said no to the scarcity myth and figured out what enough looked like for me, rather than falling into the trap of always wanting more.

If happiness for you is the accumulation of a massive amount of wealth, to use toward whatever end goal your heart desires, my blessings to you. In fact, I want to do the exact same thing. My wish is for clarity of purpose, and for you to possess the tools and freedom to follow your inner voice using empathy.

My pursuit of empathy has helped me develop some

understanding of the origins of our scarcity mindset, a topic I encourage my readers to continue to unpack on their own. The first explanation that resonated for me is that it is a derivative of the Pangea effect.

Our modern calendar and measurement systems were developed by our hunter-gather ancestors across the world. In places like Europe, societies developed in a colder climate where the growing seasons were short and fixed before a cold winter set in, when they experienced frequent periods of famine or food shortages. As a result of short growing periods and these instances of famine and food shortages, societies were forced to store food and resources for the winter and compete for the best lands and resource reserves. Our cycles of active and economic war generally stem from a grab for resources that are perceived as key for survival.

The next explanation that resonated for me has to do with how our industrial and capitalist global economy has responded to poverty and resource needs around the world. In 2010, the American Sociological Association published a report entitled "The Scarcity Fallacy."[1] It begins,

For the first time in human history, the world is home to more than one billion hungry people. New data from the United Nations suggest that a higher proportion of the Earth's people are hungry now than just a decade ago, the reverse of a long and otherwise positive trend.

The report goes on to explore the conventional wisdom that world hunger exists because of population growth, natural disasters, and shortfalls in food production, and that these stressors on resources escalate

1. Stephen J. Scanlan, J. Craig Jenkins, and Lindsey Peterson, "The Scarcity Fallacy," *Contexts* 9, no. 3 (February 1, 2010): 34–39, https://journals.sagepub.com/doi/pdf/10.1525/ctx.2010.9.1.34.

due to climate change and global warming. Ultimately, these prove to be false narratives. Even with the changes in climate, the report finds that it is actually "social inequalities, distribution systems, and other economic and political factors that create barriers to food access." This is a shining example of how a scarcity mindset fails us.

But when you look at the global food supply and the organizations that both supply food and shape polices, they have been traditionally doing so believing that more food is needed. And yet, "The Scarcity Fallacy" clearly states,

On a per capita basis, food is more plentiful today than any other time in human history . . . over the last several decades food production . . . and the average daily food availability per capita have grown, outpacing what has been the most rapid expansion of the human population ever . . . [E]ven in times of localized production

shortfalls or regional famines, there has long been a global food surplus.[2]

The idea that there is not enough food breeds more production, marketing, and logistics issues. Food supply then becomes market-based and costly. Food production increases successfully, yet all the resources are feeding production, not access. This model of food production, rooted in scarcity, is a self-defeating proposition because food remains inaccessible to those who need it most. Hence, more than a billion people continue to go hungry.

The challenges in our food supply models is just one example of how actions rooted in scarcity limit our imaginations. Our focus on producing more blinds us from the surplus that we have. There is evidence all around us that we have access to more than we acknowledge

207

2. Scanlan, Jenkins, and Peterson, "The Scarcity Fallacy," 35.

and that, individually and collectively, we can survive on less. Our basic needs for survival include food, water, shelter, and safety. There are 37 million people in the US (11 percent) and more than 700 million people globally (9.3 percent) living without access to these basic needs according to the World Bank.[3] And that's just our material needs. Our psychological needs include our relationships with our families and friends, as well as with ourselves, our purpose, and our accomplishments.

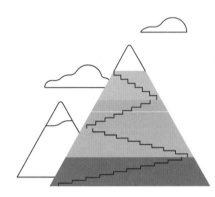

Perhaps the most famous researcher of our psychological needs is Dr. Abraham Harold Maslow, who was best known

for categorizing human needs in a hierarchy that prioritizes survival and psychological safety. In Maslow's Hierarchy of Needs—visualized as a pyramid depicting the spectrum of human needs, both physical and psychological—if a pressing need arises in the lower levels of the hierarchy, it will have to be mostly satisfied before someone could give their attention to the next highest need. The first four levels are known as deficit needs, or D-needs. The bottom or base level includes a human being's "Basic or Physiological Needs": food, water, sleep, sex, homeostasis, and excretion. On the second

3. On the population, see U.S. Census Bureau, *Current Population Survey (CPS), Annual Social and Economic Supplements (CPS ASEC): Report P60-277*, 2021, https://www2.census.gov/programs-surveys/cps/techdocs/cpsmar21.pdf, last accessed January 12, 2023; and *Poverty in the United States, 2021*, September 2022, https://www.census.gov/content/dam/Census/library/publications/2022/demo/p60-277.pdf, last accessed January 12, 2023. On basic needs, see World Bank Group, *Correcting Course: Poverty and Shared Prosperity 2022*, 15, https://openknowledge.worldbank.org/bitstream/handle/10986/37739/9781464818936ov.pdf.

> ## "Our pursuit of status and level of success deepens our sense of safety and belonging."

level are our "Safety Needs": security, order, and stability. We each need to meet our Basic Needs and our Safety Needs in order to survive.

Individuals equipped with sustenance, shelter, and safety will then attempt to fulfill their third-level needs, which fall into a category Maslow called "Love and Belonging." These are our psychological needs to connect and share ourselves with others, such as our family, friends, and romantic partners.

The fourth level is the "Esteem" level. It's human nature to pursue the feeling of competency and, even further, recognition. Our pursuit of status and level of success deepens our sense of safety and belonging. Esteem is an important layer of human need that many of us aren't given freely, and therefore struggle to give freely to others without feeling fear or jealousy.

Once our need for esteem is satisfied, we have greater access to the "Cognitive" level of need. Cognitive needs refer to our desire for intellectual challenge and exploration. We also experience "Aesthetic Needs," our human desire for beauty. At the top of the pyramid, we come to the "Need for Self-Actualization." This need is met when individuals find fulfillment in reaching toward their full potential.

Throughout this book, we've added tools to attend to our physical and emotional needs. We have the ability to focus our attention on satisfying our true lower order needs first, turning away from esteem and aesthetics until our basic needs feel securely met. From that place of safety, we can apply greater intentionality to our pursuit of purpose and accomplishment, as well as how we show up for the people that matter most to us. It's upon this foundation of satisfied needs and desires that we are equipped to pursue that which will give us a sense of fulfillment and

209

happiness. Maslow described these highest level pursuits as self-actualization.

We also have the ability to identify false needs. These are generated through our own sense of scarcity or from the projection of scarcity onto us by the outside world.

The misguided attention to possessions and titles that I once held was the source of much of the unhappiness in my life. It was when I used empathy to find the clarity and freedom to pursue love and connection, and my ideas and dreams, that I began to feel at peace and abundant. I began the increasingly easeful journey of mastery of my own potential.

DAY 21

Exercise

On Day 21, we'll practice identifying scarcity beliefs in the world around us. To release them, we must gently honor the role they've played in our lives and our sense of safety.

Today we get to externalize these myths. They no longer need to belong to you. Allow them to leave and ask that they announce themselves before they visit in the future. You can make the choice to limit or eliminate the possibility of these ideas borrowing time from you. Today, together, we establish boundaries with our scarcity myths in a ritual that helps us rewrite our own narratives.

1. Explore the areas in your own life where feeling scarcity is common. Your finances? Love life? Free time? Write a paragraph describing your experience of scarcity in each area. If any areas are missing, add them and expand

on them in a paragraph. Describe the
emotions that show up when you explore
each area of scarcity. Try to remember
the first time you had that feeling and
write it down.

2. Review the areas where you experienced the most scarcity in your life. Feel
the emotions that each area of scarcity
brought up. Where is it in your body?
Don't run away from the feelings. Express
freely any words or emotions that come
up. Don't shy away from anger, fear, sadness, or shame.

3. Grab a new piece of paper. Take a
moment to review each area of scarcity
and write a paragraph that includes
what you want. Speak into the positive
and try to be specific. For example, when
I found myself $80K in debt and running
out of money, I wrote that I wanted to
earn $100K before the end of the year
and to generate enough monthly income
to cover my costs and save aggressively.
During this step, be reasonable, but do
not limit yourself. Use the same care you
used to honor your scarcity beliefs to

honor your capabilities to achieve abundance. Describe how you want to feel when you achieve your goal. Read the list back to yourself.

4. Revisit the sheet of paper where you explored your scarcity beliefs for one final time. Find a safe place where you can burn these pages. Perhaps on a clear concrete street or in a pot that you aren't afraid to damage. As you burn the paper, say the words, "I honor my scarcity beliefs for the role they've played in protecting me. They are no longer mine. I release them to make room for my purpose and my dreams."

5. Read the positive statements you wrote in step 3 out loud to yourself and then to someone else you love. Save your affirmations somewhere you can reference when you need a reminder of your healing, your vision, your abundance, and your strength.

DAY 22
Abundance Brainstorm

What is guaranteed to bring you happiness? How do you know?

There may not be any one thing, person, or situation that is guaranteed to bring happiness. Except, as we are learning, for your own intentional actions. You are guaranteed to bring yourself happiness. When we turn toward the things that make us feel safe, seen, contented, and meaningful, we unlock greater happiness and empathy for ourselves and the world around us.

The question "What is guaranteed to bring you happiness?" was not an easy one for me to answer until recently. However, my ongoing attempts to answer the question have guided me toward appreciating the abundance in my life. Back in 2020, to practice turning away from scarcity, I contemplated the many memories, people, opportunities, and choices that contributed to who I was. Instead of focusing on the pandemic, or my unemployment, or my broken heart from losing my brothers, I turned toward my healing and spiritual growth. I turned toward my relationship with my family, my passion for fairness and entrepreneurship, and my relationships with all the people around me. Resilience and self-confidence sprang up from an internal place, and I credit this intrinsically driven happiness with everything that has unfolded in my life since then.

Today, I count among my many abundances my wife and my first child (my daughter Naya), the rest of my healthy family, my home, my businesses, my investments, and my intellectual ability to dream up and manifest more alongside people I enjoy and love. Most important among my abundances, I count my freedom and agency over how I spend my time, what I do with my body, and my ability to spend ample time with my family, to travel and work from different places around the world, and to direct my time and resources toward the spaces and causes that matter to me. These are all sources of joy. But the ability to see them and feel them started with learning to appreciate the simplest of my blessings.

A few years prior to writing this book, I was still having difficulty feeling joy. I was locked in a place of scarcity and not having enough. I had to build this muscle in me, catching the energy I spent lamenting scarcity rather than celebrating abundance, to find contentment, and eventually an overflow of happiness and possibility.

When I was unable to feel joy, it took the form of moving on very quickly from my wins and turning back to my issues and deficits. Even as the tides began to turn, I was so accustomed to feeling vulnerable, picked on, and uncertain that I always turned to the next thing rather than expressing gratitude for my achievements. This is still a challenge that I face.

My deficit of joy took the form of jealousy of others when they were happy or doing well for themselves. From a friendship and values standpoint, I felt happy for them, but deep down inside, I was comparing myself to them and feeling shame and sadness from what that assessment was telling me about myself.

When I took the time to slow down and notice what was happening, I realized that I had a hard time generating an authentic smile. My smile just didn't feel right for me, regardless of what others might be seeing on the outside. I remember feeling this way after a guided meditation when I was asked to locate the feeling of joy in my body. I felt fear, sadness, shame, and anger—but no joy. I had to learn how to find the positive feelings within me. But from desire, to knowing, to feeling, to appreciating, to amplifying, I've rewired my neural pathways to turn toward the abundance of joy that exists within me. Today, just a

215

"I magnify my own joy through advocating for safety and joy for others."

few year later, I magnify my own joy through advocating for safety and joy for others. Just by doing so, I eventually began to attract pleasant surprises along the way.

Around June of 2020, Caroline and I were establishing a new kind of routine between us while still living far apart from each other. She was in Copenhagen and I was preparing to return to NYC for the first time since the start of the COVID-19 pandemic. I had begun to receive more inquiries about our card game and my approach to spreading empathy as we began merging our commercial pursuits with activism. While we were advocating through social media, Caroline noticed an opportunity through one of her friends, Sarah Diouf, a fashion designer out of Senegal who has designed clothing worn by celebrities like Beyoncé. Sarah had shared a post from Beyoncé's stylist, Zerina Akers, who was curating a list on Beyoncé's website called the Black Parade Route,

celebrating Black makers and creatives from around the world. Caroline submitted Actually Curious for that list through an Instagram comment, and sort of forgot about it.

One day in late June of 2020, we noticed an unusual volume of purchases on the Actually Curious website. When I checked, it was coming directly from Beyoncé's website. We both investigated. We'd been featured by the Queen B herself! At that moment in time, Actually Curious had never received that level of validation. We began to brainstorm how to use the access and how to wisely use the revenue that we were generating.

Coincidentally, in April 2020, we had been contacted by a publicist who invited me to speak on a panel during Environmental Awareness Month about our efforts to make Actually Curious sustainably and to explore questions about the environment and our collective efforts to preserve it. (Yet again, by living my values I had attracted another values-aligned person.) With the ever-rising urgency of climate change and global warming, one thing we all have within our power is how and with whom we spend our money. When making Actually Curious, it was important that we found a printing partner that used recycled paper and that had extremely ethical tree harvesting and labor practices. Sustainability is important to us individually as consumers, as well as collectively as a species. A values-aligned approach to our business has helped us attract new friends that care about the same things that we do.

After the Beyoncé feature, I decided to reinvest the money we'd made to hire that publicist named Morgan to represent me and the game. Morgan was one of the fifty people I had named in my army of support brainstorm, just like the one we did together back on Day 15. I had spoken to several publicists over the course of creating Actually Curious. With Morgan, everything clicked— the timing, the resources, and most importantly, the shared understanding of what we were trying to say with my story and how it aligned with the card game and the movement to spread empathy. Together, we were able to secure a featured story in the *New York Times*, titled "How an Empathy Expert Spends His Sundays."[4] That feature tipped the pendulum of our credibility, reach, and momentum in a way that would change our material abundance significantly.

To be clear, my challenges with experiencing joy and moving to a space of honoring my resilience, cultivating grace, and showing gratitude wasn't the giant leap it may seem on paper. In reality, it was more of a gradual process—small steps to notice my habitual ways of thinking and feeling,

4. Devorah Lev-Tov, "How an Empathy Expert Spends His Sundays," *New York Times*, October 16, 2020, https://www.nytimes.com/2020/10/16/nyregion/actually-curious-michael-tennant.html.

217

honor the bad and the good, heal, and build up my gratitude muscle. The daily morning routine that was featured in that *New York Times* article helped significantly with that growth. Back then, and on most days, I work through a morning routine that consists of meditation, journaling, and reflecting on the things I'm grateful for. Often, I'll close out a journaling page with a quarter page of gratitude for any and everything I can think of. This was hard at first. It's second nature now.

When we consistently return to the things that fuel our abundance, we amplify our joy and can channel this positive energy into new ideas, relationships, projects, and ways of finding playfulness and unlocking happiness.

DAY 22
Exercise

On Day 22, together we'll practice identifying the types of abundance we have—time, attention, creativity, resources, friends, family—and use our abundance to provide a moment of joy to someone around us.

1. On a blank piece of paper, journal about all the abundance you possess in your life. Fill up the page by pushing yourself to continue finding simple things to appreciate.

2. Select three things from that list and identify the ways in which you are able to share those abundances within the next twenty-four hours. It may be as simple as celebrating this exercise in a group chat and thanking your group for being there for you.

3. Act on sharing that abundance with at least one person in the next day. Find a way to share your abundance with a

person and inspire them to notice their simple privileges.

4. Journal about how the process of noticing, prioritizing, and sharing your abundance made you feel.

DAY 23

Empathy and Abundance

Do you believe in miracles?

We've been taught that miracles, like abundance, are rare and only available to a select few. But throughout my personal journey, I've come to find that miracles are plentiful and available to all of us. Our ability to recognize miracles in our daily lives can help us move through difficult times and capture moments of gratitude that may go unnoticed or underappreciated. On Day 23, we'll dive into the practice of noticing miracles—large and small—that we are attracting through our empathy and consistency.

To explain what I mean by a "miracle," I'd like to walk you through the ones that I've been lucky enough to experience. Prior to the losses my family and I experienced, I lacked a true connection to my body, my emotions, and my values. I was sort of running on autopilot. Because I wasn't fully aware of what my body and emotions were telling me,

I'd behave outside of my own interests and well-being when I became overwhelmed by my feelings. I lacked the tools to constructively address them. Today, having the tools to stay with my emotions and listen deeply to the messages they send about my present, my past, and my future, I am able to make choices that align with my emotional needs and my values.

Back in 2019 and into 2020, these tools of self-empathy saved my life. Soon enough, I was taking care of myself and tending to my well-being. It just felt good. Situations like rejection from a job, family member, or even friend or lover allowed me to learn more about myself and about the other person. In the end, I learned to embrace the difficult emotions that arose when interacting with people. And by doing so, I learned so much about the long-term choices I needed to make for my own happiness and for each of my relationships.

A major miracle for me occurred when I learned to lean toward those honest interactions that might yield temporary discomfort but would ultimately lead to a deeper connection. I was raised in a home where the children were to be "seen and not heard" and to "speak when spoken to." This was my introduction to authoritarian power dynamics that would show up in many other places throughout my life. So my orientation in these situations has historically been toward protection and maintaining appearances, rather than connection to my inner self or safe and honest expression of difference. I count learning to recognize this—learning to forgive my parents for raising me this way, learning to forgive myself for the ways in which I rebelled against this style of parenting—as a miracle worth appreciating.

Another miracle was surviving the losses my family and I endured between 2019 and 2020. I remember the pain searing my heart for months after hearing my brother Chris had died. A pain like that serves as a reminder of the healing and resilience our hearts are capable of. Our emotional resilience as a species is a miracle and a superpower. In this book, we aim to use setbacks, losses, and traumas as a reminder that we all experience ups and downs and meet moments where we could use a bit of understanding and support.

The privilege of transforming my passions, my interests, and my purpose into commercially successful products that spread the very tools that saved me is a blessing that stems from luck, timing, and need, but also from my empathy for myself. Another miracle. The idea that by learning to love myself better, I'd unlock emotional safety, values clarity, and eventually material wealth is a miracle I could have never predicted.

Perhaps the greatest miracle is learning that I have the

power to let go of a feeling or an idea whenever I please. The control I now have over my internal narrative stems from my willingness to see the good and positive in things big and small. Miracles! Some might define them as extraordinary and welcome events that are not explicable by natural or scientific laws. A miracle can be a remarkable event or a development that brings welcome consequences. Or perhaps an exceptional product or achievement. But we can even be more liberal than this. For example, the miracle that we go to sleep every night trusting that we'll awake in the morning, and then we do. Or that, without conscious effort, our lungs will breathe, our hearts will beat, and our brains will process through all our senses.

223

DAY 23

Exercise

On Day 23, I invite you to use all that you have learned about yourself—including your body's wisdom and your values—to notice all the bounty in the world around you. Reflect on the last twenty-two days exploring the stories and lessons from this book and throughout your life, and honor all the sound choices you've made for your well-being and happiness. Think of the wonderful and memorable ways you've spent your time, and begin to imagine putting yourself in the places that felt enjoyable, productive, safe, and nourishing, with the people who excite, interest, inspire, and support you.

Are you capable of finding miracles in your daily life? On Day 23, your exercise is simple.

1. Open a note in your phone and title it "Miracle Log."

2. Start by adding any miracles that have occurred in the past twenty-two days. Be liberal with the word and see how it feels to call small moments miracles.

3. Next, open your awareness as you move through your day over the next twenty-four hours. Notice something you find beautiful in your environment or life.

4. Finally, revisit the list you've created, saying the following words before and after each miracle: "I invite miracles, big and small, into my daily life."

Strategic Applications

Where in your life do you want to apply more empathy?

A by-product of abundance is generosity. The more you use your tools of empathy, the more you will see your capacity for generosity grow. Up until this point, our practice in strengthening empathy has been focused on the self and on attuning ourselves to how our interpersonal relationships make us feel, including our families, our romantic partners, our colleagues, and our peers in our community.

We've learned how empathy for the self can lead to more intentional and impactful relationships. You will also begin to notice the generosity present in the people, organizations, and activities that you are engaged with. You will routinely find yourself the beneficiary of serendipitous moments and acts of generosity—don't question this. These are all the great benefits of living with empathy and abundance.

But there are also great possibilities for strategic impact to be made. Back on Day 3, early in our empathy journey, we learned of relationship management as one of the four components of emotional intelligence. It is the most outcome-driven component because it considers one's own emotions as well as human behavior, and it honors the ability to tend to the emotional needs of an organization to foster productivity. Now, as we arrive at Day 24, Strategic Applications, we will put relationship management into practice using our new skills in empathy on a macro level to affect long-term goal setting, clarity, consistency, and efficiency among our groups, teams, and organizations. We'll explore ways to apply what we've learned to situations where leadership is required, such as team building, teaching vulnerability, and performing diversity, equity, and inclusion work.

EMPATHY IN LEADERSHIP:
Connecting emotional awareness to the recognition of biases, executing nuanced team motivation, and fostering levity and clarity in the face of challenges and crises.

When I began to bring the Five Phases of Empathy into organizations, my goal was to help leaders gain the tools to confront emotionally charged situations with grace. Immediately, I thought back to situations I'd encountered both as a leader and as a subordinate. In most examples I came up with, I had no awareness of my own emotional state because I was too afraid or too wrapped up in my ego. I now understand why I had a feeling of dissonance from leaders who were delivering company-approved statements to rooms of young people who were concerned about their livelihood. In my reflections, I transported myself through memory and through attunement to my somatic experience, back to the "emotional containers" of my past. By the end of this book, you will be better equipped to apply your

skill in empathy to foster trust, demonstrate your commitment to respect and transparency, and honor confidentiality with individuals and among groups. You'll also be able to model and recruit associates who are capable of speaking from their own experiences and listening with curiosity. A strong emotional container is a space that encourages all in the community to bring their wisdom forward.

However, this idea also works on an individual level when preparing for group leadership. In preparation for a difficult but necessary conversation with my team, I created a container within myself to travel back in time to the "fire drill" moments of corporate layoffs. During my morning meditation session, I took care to imagine the situation in detail.

The office I was in. The people I remembered observing or gossiping with. The looks on people's faces as I walked past offices as groups mourned the layoff of a beloved colleague. I observed the fear in myself and in others, and how difficult it was to remain vulnerable in times of heightened stress. In some cases, I saw leaders using stress and fear as a motivational or productivity tool. If vulnerability wasn't being cultivated, modeled, and encouraged, how would a group have the muscle memory to be open or vulnerable in a time of heightened emotions? Short answer: They wouldn't.

In situations where evaluation, assessment, or conflict is involved, the leaders I had worked with—and the leader I had been—had always retreated to secrecy, control, and personal risk mitigation, rather than openness, group problem-solving, and shared accountability. I also observed that when it came to unconscious bias, some leaders would create a reality forcefield out of fear of judgment and shut down any topic that questioned their merit or integrity.

I want us to explore the subtle and passive fears that entrench our power structures and reinforce the inequities within our contact zones. To create a long-term effect on the systems that govern the world, we must strengthen the abilities of individual leaders to recognize the inconsistencies between their values and their practice, and grant them the emotional proficiency to confront those inconsistencies constructively. Leaders who can honor the entire spectrum of their emotions, including fear, shame, sadness, and anger, are more adept at lowering their egos and attuning to the situations and people they encounter.

EMPATHY IN TEAM BUILDING:
Fostering safety, inclusivity, and connection to create more trusting and collaborative teams.

When we model vulnerability and bring personal attunement into situations with consistency, we begin to organically see a difference in trust within ourselves as well as within groups. The skills and tools that we have practiced over the past twenty-three days can be used proactively to great effect in building team trust, chemistry, conflict-resolution skills, and resilience through challenges.

Reflective questions can have a disarming and unifying effect. Many of the organizations that I've met through Actually Curious start team meetings by pulling a question from one of the decks and offering space for the group to share their answers and perspectives. It is an easy way to slow down and check in on a human level before diving into work. As simple as it may seem, many of us are constantly running through our own loops of to-dos and internal narratives, and we sometimes forget to check in with ourselves and one another. Simply by introducing and modeling this ritual, we start to weave the fibers of connection in a group into a tight-knit fabric. Check-in moments are also a way of practicing one's own ability to lead with vulnerability. As an introverted person who struggles with anxiety, I find that frequent practice with reflective questions has helped me build my confidence and establish new awareness and constructive relationships with my anxiety.

Let's consider the advanced exercises that you have learned up to this point that you can now bring into a group setting. In Phase One, the Language of Feelings, in addition to learning how empathy works and how it can be applied, you learned a simple game that teaches you how to become more aware of your emotions and the physical responses they create. We called this exercise Feelings Roulette; others have called it the Feelings Game. It is a fun exercise that takes people out of their comfort zone and encourages them to slow down and attune to themselves and other people.

In Phase Two, the Importance of Intention, we learned how to use our values and purpose statements to help translate our emotional responses into messages from our inner voices. You thought about how your values might be influenced by the external world and were provided with an exercise that helps you assess your own values.

Long before I began my journey into writing *The Power of Empathy*, I'd used the values exercise to create greater alignment between organizations and their employees and partners. I also used the values exercise to help individuals generally act with more intention in all groups they were part of. In fact, as I noted throughout the book, the values exercise played a major part in the history of my organization, Curiosity Lab. We employed it within the organizations we've supported with brand and community-building strategies. Group values exercises are a phenomenal way to share with your teams the importance of integrity and intentionality, but also to weave intention toward shared values into the fabric of your teams and organization.

In Phase Three, Channeling Purpose, we learned exercises that strengthen our attunement in situations and in groups, like the Third Body Exercise. It was designed to help strengthen our perspective-taking abilities. When we speak on behalf of a group, we need to be aware of the various individual, situational, and societal contexts at play.

Once we have better attunement to ourselves, we can more
accurately attune to others. By
teaching and modeling this

level of awareness, you begin to
organically spread empathetic
leadership among your peers,
subordinates, and leaders.

EMPATHY IN TEACHING VULNERABILITY:
Exploring authentic, proactive, and situationally
appropriate vulnerability and understanding
how to strategically model vulnerability in
communities and organizations.

In organizations of the past
and present, vulnerability has
been seen as a liability and a
weakness. It is common for
a leader to scold colleagues
for mistakes rather than get
curious about what might
prove to be a growth opportunity for the company or organization. In addition, less than
empathetic work interactions
foster a fear of questioning
authority. An expression of
curiosity, in many cases, might
be seen as a lack of faith in the
decision-making of leadership,
and therefore not encouraged
or tolerated.

We hide our vulnerability to
protect our egos and our

power. When we hide ourselves
and our need for support in
organizational settings, the
effect on individuals and the
culture of the community is
long term. But vulnerability
often leads to connection. In
the 2021 Ernst & Young Empathy in Business Survey,[5] which
tracks how empathy affects
leaders, employees, and innovation in the workplace, it was
found that "90 percent of US
workers believe empathetic
leadership leads to higher
job satisfaction"; "88 percent

---

5. Lizzie McWilliams, "New EY Consulting Survey
Confirms 90% of US Workers Believe Empathetic
Leadership Leads to Higher Job Satisfaction and
79% Agree It Decreases Employee Turnover,"
Ernst & Young (press release), October 14, 2021,
https://www.ey.com/en_us/news/2021/09
/ey-empathy-in-business-survey.

feel that empathetic leadership creates loyalty among employees toward their leaders"; and "79 percent agree it decreases employee turnover." As it turns out, having leaders who are capable of fostering a safe space for vulnerability is important to the bottom line.

When there is no safety to express our vulnerabilities, we eventually feel unsafe in our communities and environments. An awareness of body language and the overall energy in the room can help you identify when safety is strained and vulnerability is inaccessible. I often remind myself that when I feel something, there is a good chance that it is real. You can deepen the safety of the room or emotional container simply by sharing what you observe and how it makes you feel, and asking if anyone feels the same. An example of this might be saying, "I notice the room is quieter than normal, and I believe I see concern on faces. I feel concern as well and wanted to bring it out into the open. Is anyone feeling the same or differently?"

Simply by noticing, acknowledging, and sharing the emotional qualities of what you are experiencing, you model vulnerability so others can do the same. As others share, you'll notice how the feeling in the room changes, and how the feeling in yourself changes as well. Begin to notice how vulnerability relates to abundance. On the other side of fear and vulnerability are usually bravery, pride, connection, and growth. It costs you nothing to flex this muscle, yet the benefits are innumerable and priceless.

EMPATHY IN DIVERSITY, EQUITY, AND INCLUSION WORK:
Introducing new tools and skills for the continuation and practice of difficult but necessary conversations.

Lastly, I want to underscore that all the knowledge, skills, and tools that we've learned and practiced to increase our own capacities for empathy organically make us better allies for any cause that we touch. Diversity, equity, and inclusion has always been an area of focus for me, as I have benefited from the bravery and innovation that created opportunities for me. These opportunities have also given me a firsthand seat to watch as the emotions of fear, sadness, shame, and anger can serve to impede diversity, equity, inclusion, and justice (DEIJ) progress by entrenching the historic privilege and bias that exist within our societal structures.

My work in corporate DEIJ and empathy training began from a simple insight. When the ego is threatened, conflict mitigation and the redressing of inequities become psychologically unsafe for leaders and power holders. This work threatens the status quo and at times the personal material abundance and sense of merit of the very people it seeks to educate. When we ask the beneficiaries of power imbalances to repair those power imbalances, it can feel to them like we're asking them to inflict harm on themselves. Natural defenses kick in, preventing us from going any further. Confronting one's own ego or unconscious biases works in this same exact way.

During well-intentioned efforts to support diversity, equity, inclusion, and justice, our groups encounter the societal narratives around scarcity that we explored earlier: the belief that for others to gain safety, access, and privileges, those

233

things must be taken away from their current holders. We need leaders who can create the containers to bring these organizational myths into open discussion. The ideas and emotions that surface in these settings only serve to activate the ego and shut down the curiosity of the groups that need this work most. *The Power of Empathy* means to inspire more emotionally proficient leaders who can navigate toward harmony. It means to build equity from the inside out, teaching the knowledge and tools necessary to challenge internal and external narratives so that we can challenge systems of power from a mindset of abundance.

These are just a few tangible ways that empathy can be used to proactively build safety and to motivate individuals and groups, but really the possibilities are endless. With empathy, a new orientation to the world that brings clarity to individual contentment and desire is possible. This vantage point becomes a place of strength to allow more secure and compassionate movement throughout the world. It all begins with you.

DAY 24

Exercise

On Day 24, I invite you to develop a mood board to inspire you to foster greater empathy in your Circles of Control and Influence—self, family, friends, work, school, and community. Remember, your intentional efforts in your Circles of Control expand your Circle of Influence and affect how you experience and respond to your Circle of Concern. Take a moment to fill out the following chart and begin to form your own strategy for applying empathy in your world this year and beyond.

WAYS YOU INTEND TO APPLY GREATER EMPATHY IN YOUR CIRCLES OF CONTROL:

Self

Family

School/Work

Community

Leadership

Relationships

Vulnerability

Purpose

Manifestation

236

What miracles do you want to manifest in this life by using the power of empathy?

By this point in our journey, I'm making the assumption that you, too, believe in miracles. But if you are still on the fence, that is OK. All I ask is that for the remainder of our journey, you suspend your disbelief and join me in entertaining the following assumptions: First, we will define the word *miracle* as "an extraordinary event, development, or accomplishment that brings very welcome consequences."[6] Second, we will assume that we are all good people worthy of experiencing miracles in our lifetimes. And third, we'll move forward with the belief that miracles are abundant, or even infinite, and all we need to do to experience them is to invite them into our lives.

In the past, if I were in your shoes, I'd likely tune out at the frequent mention of miracles. I'm a cynical New Yorker who grew up in Bed-Stuy in the '80s. While I haven't lived the most at-risk and under-resourced life, I have experienced hardships that, for a time, left me feeling more skeptical than optimistic about life. My parents lived through more difficult circumstances than I did, and many people who I grew up with faced even tougher hardships. When you have faced difficult circumstances or know others who have, the idea of miracles can feel like fantasy when up against the realities of day-to-day life.

Without adequate infrastructure and with few tools for recognizing and healing from our current and historical trauma, it is no wonder that a dominant feature of life for many people is suffering. We witness individuals, communities, and nations experiencing pain and trauma in the news on a day-to-day basis. It would be naive to extol

---

6. Sister Jan Craven, "Definition of a Miracle," Sisters of Providence of Saint Mary of the Woods, 2015, https://spsmw.org/2015/08/18/definition -of-a-miracle/.

the existence of infinite miracles and abundance without acknowledging this reality for most people. But when scarcity becomes the dominant belief system, it has a funny way of manifesting itself and creating inertia. If we believe that the things we need are scarce and rare, then they become scarce and rare. Let's test this idea.

What are among the scarcest and rarest desired objects in our society? Money, food, medicine, love, trust, possessions? You name it. If you are challenged to look, you'll find instances where objects of our desire, like love and trust, are abundantly available to us when we open ourselves to finding them. Objects like money, food, and medicine are available to our species in abundance, yet they are hoarded out of fear that the surplus will be required later for survival and happiness. And you need only visit your own closet or, more dramatically, the local junkyard, or even the estate sale of someone recently deceased, to see the fleeting value of many of the possessions we once coveted.

Let's look at this another way by examining the truth in the scarcity of miracles. Miracles exist in our society in the rare form that they do because we, as a society, choose to view miracles as scarce and elusive. Most of us have accepted the religiously and artistically scaled idea that miracles are the realm of privileged magic. Stuff reserved for the gods, demigods, prophets, and the chosen among us. Those who are blessed to be touched by miracles reap riches and rewards. Those who are blessed to be touched by a miracle are exalted in sacred books and fabled stories. In some ways, those who experience miracles have their names live on in eternity. Who wouldn't want to hold such power? I know who wouldn't: those who live with open hearts and trust in the power of empathy.

237

"Each of us has the ability to manifest changes in our present reality."

Manifestation works when you choose to believe that you are worthy of your dreams and desires becoming true. And perhaps some of you have adopted my naive dream of inspiring happiness, well-being, and the sharing of abundance.

Earlier in the book, we spoke about Circles of Influence and Circles of Concern. Ideas, emotions, dreams, and wishes are very similar in quality to miracles, and they are in our control. They are abstractions that exist in the mind. But by channeling our energy into those ideas, and realizing them through choices and actions, we manifest them into the physical world. In that sense, manifestation is simply the awareness that what we think of, and give energy to, becomes our reality.

Each of us has the ability to manifest changes in our present reality, but it requires awareness, choice, consistency, and surrendering. I use the word *surrender* because this is the part that might seem

to sit in the realm of magic. Manifestation starts and stops with the genuine belief that you deserve the idea or object of your desire. This pursuit of believing, on a deeply felt level, that we are worthy is the key to manifesting our dreams and desires. It takes empathy for yourself and for others to return over and over again to the blessed gift of manifesting our dreams.

I manifest the spreading of empathy because I choose to believe that my purpose on this earth at this moment is to use my freedom and resources toward this goal. The moment I stop believing in that purpose, or stop being able to support this mission, my energy will stop being channeled in that direction. And in that case, perhaps it would be too late to stop the movement, because it would have spread beyond me and those I am able to know in my lifetime.

Examples of manifestation are all around us if we train our

eyes to see them. Manifestation exists in the physical world, in art and inventions. Something that never existed before is imagined and manifested in this world by a person or people. The card game Actually Curious was a manifestation of the shared values, beliefs, and ideas of the people at Curiosity Lab in the summer of 2018. Manifestations also exist in the abstract world, as seen in the feeling evoked by a poem, or a song, or even by the jealous expectations of a crossed lover. The feelings one person or group had, imagined having, or tried to convey through some form of expression—physical, audible, sensory—is actually experienced by others.

When your idea of what will happen turns out to be true, this is a form of manifestation. We might call it a prediction, luck, or chance, when in fact we hold more power and agency than we give ourselves credit for. Words and ideas have power. By fixing our thoughts on an idea or outcome, we

subconsciously lead ourselves to that idea or outcome. When our idea of what might happen turns out to be true and it's a pleasant thing, we credit our luck. In this case, it is possible that we had information that helped us deduce this possible outcome logically. Psychic ability is unlikely, though we might playfully assert otherwise. It is equally likely that we will ourselves toward the outcome, subconsciously playing a hand in making the prediction come true.

When our idea of what will happen turns out to be true and it's an unpleasant thing, we are quick to celebrate our prediction or deflect accountability elsewhere in the form of complaints or gossip. Celebrating a prediction gives you control in the past: "Aha, I knew it. I'm smart." And deflecting accountability elsewhere gives some immediate emotional comfort—"See? It's their fault that I feel this way about what happened"—while obstructing any learning or growth that

239

might be achieved. Isn't it also possible that we surrender our agency when we put too much energy into negative predictions? We leave things to chance instead of helping them along—or worse, we actively invite failure because it's what we think we deserve.

As I write this, I can feel my mind calling bullshit on these hypotheticals. In my personal development work, I'm still practicing trust, optimism, and the willingness to be wrong or surrender control. Through curiosity and empathy, I am aware that I typically find safety in taking the position that colored my youth—realistic pessimism is my inclination. It is not comfortable for me, even today, to surrender to the belief that what I truly desire will be provided for me.

It is with deep self-compassion for the life journey we all experience that I offer my compassion to those who are seeking peace, safety, well-being, and happiness. It is with this awareness that I surrender to sharing and learning through the work of empathy. It is with the tools of somatic awareness and the clarity of my values and purpose that I translate my spectrum of emotions—joy, fear, anger, shame, and sadness—into my personal blueprint for happiness and fulfillment.

Let's examine a few other examples of manifestation.

When someone comes up with an idea and takes ten years to bring it to a point of being, this, too, is a form of manifestation. We might call it grit or resilience, and it is. But that extended manifestation is just as remarkable as an unexpected miracle, so long as the pursuit and result of the pursuit brings about happiness and fulfillment for those involved. What greater miracle exists than having the safety and means of pursuing an idea that brings you joy, and then to see it manifest into a version of itself that you've always dreamed? No matter how long that takes, the feeling is immeasurable, addictive, and repeatable. When you manifest your dreams from a deeply felt place, you know what to do at all phases of the journey, because you're bringing about this reality with every thought and action that you commit energy to.

When someone takes an inherited fortune and multiplies it, even this is a form of manifestation. We might call it privilege or luck. Because we are colored by a history of scarcity mindset, when someone else has abundance and we don't, it is common for us to envy that person and channel our attention to the roadblocks that exist in our own lives that we assume may not have existed in theirs. This viewpoint, which I, too, catch myself falling into, takes us away from agency and curiosity and into comparison and jealousy. Instead of coming up with a way of understanding the person, what their path really was, and what we might learn from their journey, we direct energy toward our narratives of pain and disadvantage. That energy could easily be channeled toward small incremental steps that bring you closer to your desires. Instead of channeling our emotions into slander and gossip, we might view this multiplying of wealth as the result of generations of accumulative manifestation. It's a ripple effect that we, too, can create. Accumulative manifestation starts with ourselves and our loved ones and ripples out as far as our presence allows.

DAY 25

On Day 25, we'll practice stating our wishes for abundance in the world.

1. Develop a specific wish list for things you want to see in the world or in your life.

2. List your limiting beliefs around these wishes on a separate piece of paper.

3. Find a safe space outside away from the building, dry grass, or paper, and ceremonially burn the list of limiting beliefs.

4. As it burns, say these words: "I surrender my choice and my past narratives in order to manifest my version of abundance."

PHASE SIX
Sharing Our Gifts

Congratulations, you've completed the Five Phases of Empathy program, designed to help you unlock greater well-being, empathy, and abundance in your life.

I received this calling back in 2020 and have accepted the responsibility of sharing what I've learned with the world. When I began seeking to spread empathy, I realized I unconsciously stepped into the role of facilitator in many settings. This became apparent to me in the exhaustion I'd feel for days after hosting an empathy workout public training or a corporate event. After reaching out to the mentors who supported me as I ventured deeper into sharing these tools, I learned that I was retraumatizing myself in the process of supporting others.

The work I was doing to support others through conflict and healing was exposing how much work I still needed to do on myself. As I transported myself back to my childhood,

exposed community violence and neglect, and called out the culture of shame that my parents experienced and fostered, I realized that the little boy within me still has parts to heal. It took several moments of inexplicable discomfort to learn that supporting the healing of others helps me heal from my own trauma. I have compassion for the child within each person I meet, because I know that most of what we experienced as children happened to us, not through us. I know this because I have a vulnerable relationship with my own need for healing. I've been able to support my inner child by offering gentle compassion, as well as the leadership and protection to relive painful moments, survive them, and alter my neurological memory to be more resilient.

As conscious and empathetic human beings, we have a choice: We can heal, or we can perpetuate and pass down our trauma. We can turn toward compassion for ourselves and others, or we can turn toward

"You want to support the healing of others because it amplifies your own!"

judgment and the perpetuation of distance, letting the walls we build around our trauma keep other people at a distance.

That is the message of Phase Six and this book. When you commit to having empathy for yourself and commit to your own healing, your compassion grows. You cannot help but see the pain you've endured present in the people and situations around you. You want to support the healing of others because it amplifies your own!

When I first chose to listen to my intrinsic voice and design the Five Phases of Empathy, I didn't have a strategy or plan or vision for how I would share this gift with the world. It happened organically. I had to do the work, many times over, of understanding how trusting this progression of living and being would yield the outcomes I truly desired. Even today, I have to practice and course correct when I find myself acting, thinking, or feeling something that is driven by

my trauma, other people's trauma, or some kind of need for external validation or ingrained scarcity belief.

While speaking and teaching about empathy, I was forced to deepen my learning. Through books, articles, documentaries, lectures, and countless conversations and workshops with people just like you, I began to see empathy in everything I encountered: my sources of support, the mirrors of my actions and desires, the next generation that will walk in my shoes. There are opportunities to learn, receive, and share tools of empathy all around us. Even if you only share your empathy with one person, your impact on them will make ripples further than you can see. The presence and energy we put out into the world changes the world.

It's a noble but challenging act to share our gifts of empathy. By doing so, we hold space for the experiences of others in varying forms. There will be times where people you care about will trust you to hold their deepest pains and their darkest secrets. Perhaps even more challenging, if you find yourself moderating difficult but necessary conversations among strangers, you may encounter thoughts and opinions that trigger powerful emotions inside you.

Let's take it to another level and imagine that while you are aiming to protect the safety of a container or third body, a comment someone made has triggered you and others in the group. How do you handle this situation? I remember the first time I encountered this situation. There was a seemingly well-intentioned white man who was speaking longer than anyone else on the video call and saying phrases and labels that offended others in the group. I could tell by the facial expressions as I scanned the faces. People turned off their videos as he spoke. I had no idea what to do.

In Phase Six, I will provide some advance preparation for emotionally charged situations that you might encounter on your journey into spreading the tools of empathy, and strategies for how to remain resilient through the inevitable stumbles.

I decided to write this sixth phase because I remember the days and weeks of exhaustion I felt upon encountering situations where I felt attacked, disrespected, disregarded, or diminished. I was learning how to maintain my grace and when to lean into greater emotion to teach, model, and demonstrate how to live with empathy. I had to learn how to remain grounded in my integrity and intention in any group. I had to learn how to release the energy I took in while running these groups, and to get support unpacking, learning from, and clearing the emotions I felt. Frankly, there were times when I was feeling burnt out or physically unwell.

My empathy journey informed me that living by the power of empathy, and leaning further to share that work, would require expanding my knowledge of self-care, facilitation, and energy management. I had to listen to my somatic experience, release assumptions, and respond to my body's needs with rest and gentle inquiry on a moment-to-moment basis. I sought mentors in the fields of emotional healing, trauma-informed facilitation, and mindfulness to help me deepen my knowledge and anticipation of what might happen in my workshops, as well as tools for how to handle my own reactions and those of the individuals and groups I encountered. I began to investigate and sign up for bodywork and Reiki energy treatments to help me recover and to learn to cleanse myself of the external energies I was taking on while facilitating. I had to protect myself and those I would be supporting as I moved toward expanding my compassion and opening up to share love and support more freely.

Phase Six, Sharing Our Gifts, is for readers who want to do more—who want to use their empathy to enact wider change in the world while remaining resilient in the process. In Phase Six, I put a finer point on the need for healing from trauma. I'll illustrate how facilitating and teaching the exploration of empathy helps deepen our own healing and growth, as we learn to overcome each new challenge. Finally, I'll offer permission to make empathy and curiosity a lifelong ritual by aspiring toward the pursuit of mastery and the humility of a beginner's mind. No matter your purpose for using your deepened skill in empathy, the knowledge and tools you learn will support you along the way.

Healing with Empathy

What are you still working to heal from?

Take your time with this question. There is no rush. You have the tools to support your inquiry, your findings, and your own healing. You have the awareness and courage to seek support. Many of our peers want this awareness and courage as well but don't know where to start. You also have the capacity to share empathy and compassion with others who surround you. Your willingness to go deeper within your own emotional awareness, presence, healing, and growth expands your ability to support others, and your process of sharing support deepens your ability to receive it. On Day 26, we explore and commit to the cycle of collective healing in whatever form is authentic to us or needed based on our individual situations.

My story is just one example of how someone becomes aware of pain and trauma, and how they subtly sabotage a person's ability to live the life they desire. Our traumas keep us stuck in moments of the past that need to be healed. They influence our emotions in situations we encounter throughout our lives. What we don't heal, we relive, and then pass along. It took meeting my emotional rock bottom to start my climb back up, but your process of radical self-empathy can start at any point. As I gained a willingness to support myself and support others, my ability to experience all emotions deepened. I learned how to truly connect. How to understand. And ultimately, how to let go.

In many ways, I was one of the lucky ones. I was able to survive and live a high-functioning life despite the trauma that I experienced as a child. Since 1995, when a groundbreaking study was conducted by the Centers for Disease Control and the Kaiser Permanente health care organization in California, education and public health researchers have been screening for ACEs, or

247

adverse childhood experiences, in children under the age of eighteen. The now widely adopted screening method looks for three categories, or ten specific kinds, of adversities that children might face in the home environment, including various forms of physical and emotional abuse, neglect, and household dysfunction. The study found ACEs to be extremely common, with more than two-thirds of the population reporting having experienced one ACE, and nearly a quarter having experienced three or more. Additionally, there's a powerful, persistent correlation between the number of ACEs experienced and the chance of poor outcomes later in life, including dramatically increased risk of heart disease, diabetes, obesity, depression, substance abuse, smoking, poor academic achievement, time out of work, and early death.[1]

I learned about ACEs only months before losing my two brothers, both of whom were under the age of fifty. Both died of heart conditions. Both suffered from diabetes and obesity. I know both had experienced traumatic events throughout their lives, and that neither received support as children or adult men to process and heal from that trauma. Processing and healing were not traits or habits that we inherited.

One of the biggest generational traits I needed to unlearn was fear of vulnerability. I would keep my feelings bottled up. And, by extension, I would project my feelings away from myself by blaming and shaming others. This way of relating was entrenched in trauma, and not just personal trauma—it was bolstered by inherited generational remnants from systems of patriarchy, colonialism, slavery, and systemic separation of

1. Centers for Disease Control and Prevention and Kaiser Permanente, *The ACE Study Survey Data* [Unpublished Data]. Atlanta, GA: US Department of Health and Human Services,

Centers for Disease Control and Prevention, 2016, https://www.cdc.gov/violenceprevention/aces /about.html.

family groups. These systems used physical and psychological abuse to control individuals and populations. I would bring a trauma of internalized shame and verbal abuse into so many relationships—romantic, familial, professional. As I learned to let go, I started creating the space for and seeking the knowledge I needed to recreate myself. When I stopped committing energy to negative guilt- and regret-infused narratives, I was able to reallocate that time and energy to my values, ideas, and beliefs.

Humans have the remarkable ability to heal from our emotional scars. We will all experience the loss of a person we love, and we will all have the opportunity to recover and carry on. In carrying on, however, we are changed because the physical world that supported us has changed. When we make our way through these moments of loss and grief, we bring wisdom along with us. It's never easy, so I offer the light at the end of the tunnel to help. Regardless of where you are in life experience, with love, grace, patience, and acceptance, you will heal at your own pace. Once you do, I hope that you will find the capacity to support another person, or a great many people, as they encounter their own challenges.

When supporting and understanding our loved ones, colleagues, and the strangers we encounter in our lives, it is inevitable that we will encounter individuals who are struggling to recover from trauma. I invite you to embrace the challenge to support them. Our work as empathetic leaders is not meant to take the place of professional therapy. We are not medically trained. However, the gift and practice of checking in with ourselves and one another can go a long way toward putting ourselves and the people we care about on the path to what's needed. A simple empathetic action can offer meaningful support in a critical time of need.

249

But how do we know if we have the capacity to support? When we heal our own trauma, we create that supportive space and deepen our firsthand knowledge of how best to help. I've come to learn that the path to healing is being able to fully experience the trauma from which we've suffered until we reach a place of completion.

Conceptually, the path to healing from trauma has three stages: establishing safety, retelling the story of the traumatic event, and reconnecting. Establishing safety begins by focusing on control of the body and gradually moves outward toward control of the environment. Survivors often feel unsafe in their bodies. Their emotions and their thinking feel out of control. This can lead to various forms of bodily neglect or toxic ways of coping. Safety is crucial because the second stage, retelling the traumatic event, is the longest and most unpredictable part.

In a 2002 research project entitled "Recovery from Psychological Trauma,"[2] Dr. Judith Herman of Cambridge Hospital describes the second stage of recovery as a period of mourning that "feels like a surrender to endless tears." But, as she reminds us, the process is temporary and its intensity diminishes over time as it becomes a memory.

Finally, the third stage of trauma recovery is reconnection with oneself and ordinary life. Herman notes that the "survivor has regained some capacity for appropriate trust." This is as much about trust in oneself as it is in other people. It's when you know you can move on with your life, and with establishing relationships, feeling normal again outside of the trauma that was experienced.

This is not an easy process. It must be met with patience and

2. Judith L. Herman, "Recovery from Psychological Trauma," *Psychiatry and Clinical Neurosciences* 52 (January 4, 2002): S98–S103, https://doi.org/10.1046/j.1440-1819.1998.0520s5S145.x.

grace. We all heal at our own pace. Where you are able, really sink into the emotions that come up. Seek support. Ask to be held, physically and figuratively. This might be a simple as asking for a hug from someone you care about who can help create the safety you need to start the process. It also might mean enlisting the help of a therapist or other professional who can work with you on this part of your journey.

We all have our love languages. We each give and receive safety and love differently, which means we can tailor our love and support based on the person or situation. In many situations, sharing and receiving words of affirmation or quality time may be what is required. In other more intimate situations, a gift, an act of service, or reassuring touch may be what does the trick.

Once safety is established to revisit traumatic experiences, we can use memories, stories, and the tools of empathy

that we've learned to support our healing. You can use this method to learn more about how you, specifically, need to be supported by others. You can also use this method to be better at supporting others. Your human instinct to support will be enhanced as you become better at both giving and receiving support.

You may notice that the people who love us naturally gather around to support us when we are hurt. Receive this! If it's hard for you to receive their support, start to practice compassion for the parts of you that don't want support. There is more to feel and to learn in all of it.

As we explored on Day 1, we act as mirrors to one another. Your work giving space to and honoring your own trauma teaches you to recognize and hold a compassionate space for the struggles of others. But to be clear, simply giving space to and honoring your own trauma might be enough for you. Knowing your limit is totally all right. We don't need to fix or be fixed all at once. Sometimes, the best path to healing begins and ends with deep acceptance. Full stop.

I had spent years trying to find the safety to commit to my healing. For me, avoiding and hiding was a fine solution, until it wasn't. I would quietly shut down when people tried to fix me. I was effective at shielding myself from many of the emotions we fear—shame, sadness, fear, anger. I had become my own barrier to experiencing deep joy and happiness. I had to learn on my own how to create the safety to feel, experience, heal, and reconnect. The by-product of getting more

comfortable at confronting my suffering, in whatever form it appeared, was that I could be present and grateful for joy and serendipity in the many forms that they appear.

On my journey to recover from trauma and addiction, I learned what it means to give myself love, attention, and space to heal. It unlocks your potential. There is nothing more powerful than feeling deeply seen and accepted in our struggles and need for support. It removes the energetic investment of hiding from that trauma. It costs us nothing but time and energy to provide this kind of support to others. The value of this healing is infinite, perpetual, and priceless.

I hope that my vulnerability in sharing the details of my struggles and my healing will give others permission to lower their ego enough to get started on their own journey of recovery.

DAY 26

For today's exercise, think of people who might benefit from your support.

1. Ask yourself these questions:

Are you willing to support someone who is suffering from trauma?

Are you able to offer empathy and not sympathy?

In what ways are you comfortable providing support?

What will you do if and when their needs are beyond your capabilities?

2. Remember: As you deepen your journey into empathy, it is important to practice empathy with yourself as well. Know your limits and capabilities, and know you have permission to help and still maintain boundaries. Plan ahead of time so you can remain grounded should your sense of safety become compromised or more challenging emotions emerge and become triggering.

3. Today, I invite you to take note of anything that has come up that you need to work with to let go. What traumas and energetic investments are holding you back from supporting others in letting go of the burdens they are ready to release? Repeat this reflection whenever you are facing a challenging moment that you need support holding space for. Share this prompt when you are supporting someone who might be facing a similar need for healing.

DAY 27

Learning Through Teaching

What do you do in your everyday life to create safer spaces for marginalized communities?

To this question, if I am honest, there have been days in the past when I would have to say "not much." It was especially so on the days when I found myself struggling to find some momentum in my life. As we learned on Day 21, Scarcity Myths, we need to take care of our basic needs for survival and our own psychological needs before we are able to lower our egos and turn our attention outward to others. My basic psychological and physical needs were met, but my sense of loving and belonging and my self-esteem had room for healing. When my physical and psychological safety were disrupted in 2019, I needed to rebuild my sense of safety from the bottom up. How could I advocate for marginalized communities when I myself was feeling vulnerable and marginalized?

This is the reason we spend so much time strengthening our self-empathy. Our ability to support others must spring from our own internal abundance. Once that gap is met internally, the support we share with others becomes an amplifier of our own happiness. It's really a bit selfish in that sense. Or more like a win-win. The individual work that we do to strengthen our self-empathy is certainly not a substitute for therapy, anti-racism training, or leadership development—but it is absolutely a complement and an amplifier.

I had attended individual psychotherapy for over a decade before I began developing and practicing the Five Phases of Empathy. I have attended various forms of group therapy and community circles, including Sunday school and Bible study at church, my weekly EVRYMAN men's group, and even periods of substance recovery group therapy. Talk therapy isn't new for me. And while understanding empathy and practicing it

255

through reflective exercises has benefited me tremendously, I've made the most progress by embracing a holistic approach. To arrive where I am today, I had to undergo my own process of grief, recovery, and acceptance of support. I denied my trauma. I got angry when people tried to help me. I bargained. I sunk into depression. And I eventually accepted myself and my need for support. With multiple modalities of support, I was able to curate my own rituals for self-empathy. It's important that you explore and find the combination that works for you. Every bit of work that you do on your own healing comes to aid you as you support yourself and others.

Over the past ten years, I've gradually deepened my meditation practice, and this has been an important part of amplifying my empathy. I started off using apps like Headspace and Calm. I now use the Insight Timer app at times or a YouTube meditation in group settings to take advantage of visual aids. About five years ago I was gifted a self-guided meditation training that changed my life. There I learned about the purpose of a mantra and simple principles of practicing and teaching meditation without aids or guidance. It was here that I learned how much I could learn by teaching. To lead a meditation, I had to learn how to be grounded enough to create a safe and meditative environment for others. It is difficult to create a space for mindfulness when you are unsettled.

In late 2019, I began using the tools I'd learned to support my own resilience, and to support my branching out to engage with others. I wanted to pay forward the support I had been fortunate enough to receive. In June of 2020, the Curiosity Lab and Actually Curious movement to spread empathy gained momentum. It was shortly after the murder of George Floyd, a lightning rod moment in a tense summer dotted with several other highly publicized murders of Black individuals. As such, our work using empathy to support healing and the facilitation of difficult but necessary topics often had us being asked to support DEIJ and anti-racism training needs. Again, here, empathy works as a complement and an amplifier.

I have many phenomenal mentors in these areas who have inspired and influenced my purpose. Mentors like Edward Gonzales, DEI lead for NASA, and Stephanie Royal, the chief people officer of the Robin Hood Foundation, the largest poverty nonprofit in New York. These leaders learned about my work and invited me to come support and teach their communities. What I learned along the way was that they and other leaders in their roles also needed support. Often they are the first or only person in their roles and must navigate the nuanced challenge of advocating for evolution and change within and throughout the organizations

and systems that finance their work. The Five Phases of Empathy is meant to support those leaders in tracking and honoring their emotional well-being and resilience.

The Five Phases of Empathy and movement to spread empathy are meant to proliferate the leaders who possess affective empathy and democratize the ability to learn it. When more people within organizations are equipped to acknowledge privileges, gaps, and bias; understand how others might be affected on an emotional level by a tough conversation; and respond to challenges with empathy and professionalism, then the job of moving inclusivity and equity forward is no longer the role of the few, or worse, the responsibility of the marginalized, but of the community as a whole. It's embedded in the culture of organizations.

While DEIJ and social responsibility are key focus areas for me and my team, tools of empathy are valuable alongside any leadership or learning and development program. The tools to recognize, be with, and confront challenging emotions translate to all phases of life. As we learned in Phase One, the Language of Feelings, when individuals and groups experience situations that involve heightened emotions, it can hinder their cognitive processing. This might surface during a work emergency, an unexpected accident involving a child or family member, or even in a community disaster. Individuals who are trained to notice emotional shifts and to self-regulate are better equipped to support others. This is true in moments of crisis as well as in day-to-day decision-making and interactions. The more people who are trained in empathy, the more people who can combine efforts to navigate the group to a place of safety, harmony, and order.

I speak from experience as an introverted leader who is overcoming my own scars from working under or alongside toxic leadership. Often I have a low capacity for holding space for all things at once—taking solitary space to write, speaking in an interview or on a podcast, meeting with current and potential clients, and also managing and mentoring our team. An ongoing audit of my emotions, energy, and rest is required for me to show up prepared and with positive and motivating energy. This kind of interrogation of the emotional quality of my exchanges, with others and with myself, helps me show up intentionally in my life. The level of self-awareness that the Five Phases of Empathy cultivates helps ensure that, as a leader, you get to show up aware, connected, composed, and prepared for the inevitable surprises that life throws at you.

"You will shift people's awareness with your ability to slow down and be present."

Once we begin to apply empathy, we see its effect and benefit on our growth goals as well as on individuals and teams with which we interact. Without even needing to train other people, you will shift people's awareness with your ability to slow down and be present, tune into your emotions, and respond with grace.

Further, if we proactively spread the tools that we are using to foster safety, openness, and connection, we enlist support in proliferating empathetic team interactions. The more we practice and surround ourselves with people who possess empathetic awareness, the more we learn about the subtle yet powerful effects this way of orienting to emotions has on individuals and situations.

Today, when I reflect on what I do to create safer spaces for marginalized communities, the responses are easy. All the work I do aims to teach the recipients and the transgressors of bias and power dynamics the skills to notice and the emotional proficiency to pursue change. I teach people to pay attention to their bodies, and the reactions of the people around them, so they recognize the opportunities to speak up.

259

DAY 27

Exercise

Day 27, Learning Through Teaching, is an invitation to allow yourself to move fluidly between the roles of student and teacher. Let this way of moderating an inner dialogue between these parts of yourself, the teacher and the student, become a playful part of your self-awareness and reflection practice. However, today we'll support you in stepping more deeply into the mindset and role of the teacher.

Today's exercise will allow you to develop more confidence in your empathy skills and thinking, and give you the tools to teach two facilitation formats to help other individuals strengthen their awareness of self and of others, as well as their emotional intelligence. I invite you to revisit the concepts and exercises you've practiced over the past twenty-six days. You are going to develop your own lesson plan. Revisit Phase One and review some of the basic knowledge and building blocks of empathy that have been useful or transformational in your own thinking and practice. These will give you facts and narratives to support your teaching, as well as help you find your own authentic way of speaking about empathy.

1. Identify the most important questions you were asked at the beginning of and throughout your empathy journey. What would you most like to share with others about your progress and process? These will become easy to recall and be among the organic ways that you can bring tools of empathy into your world and community.

As I have brought Actually Curious and the Five Phases of Empathy out into various communities, some of the questions that have proven to create meaningful dialogue include the following:

What do you love most about yourself?

What is one thing you are proud to have inherited from your parents?

What are you willing to fight for?

What is guaranteed to bring you happiness?

2. For Day 27, set an intention of bringing a thoughtful icebreaker, a unique game night, or even an empathy workshop to a loved one, cohort, or work group that is meaningful to you. And when you're ready, share a group selfie or testimonial on the *Power of Empathy* website to inspire our beautiful community of readers like yourself.

Triggers and Ego

What's something that triggers fear in you, and how does your body respond to fear?

By now you may have some answers for this question, but by no means will your audit be complete. The reason we spend so much time exploring our difficult emotions—fear, shame, sadness, and anger—is that these are the emotions most associated with our triggers. Our triggers take us out of cognitive clarity and set off impulsive emotions and actions. Those of us who lean forward into facilitating or teaching empathetic leadership will eventually encounter individuals who experience triggering reactions to questions or to the responses others share. In our journey to support others, it's very possible that we may experience triggering emotions of our own when our trauma resurfaces in a new form. In these instances, it's important to gain some practice in assessing triggering emotions and knowing what to do. On Day 28, Triggers and Ego, we explore what to do when we or the people we support experience a triggering event.

Can you recall the last time you had a triggering experience? Was it an emotional response to something that had been said or done? What physical sensations arose? What emotions can you connect to that were brought up in the moment? What past experiences remind you of that moment? I ask you this series of questions because traumatic experiences, small and large, work this way. You experience the effects of the trigger but aren't always aware of what set off the triggering experience. Even when we identify the source, we may not have clarity around what we are feeling and why. Typically, the immediate thing that triggers us relates back to similar experiences from our past. If we are able to assess the triggering experience and identify a pattern from our past, we can then begin the work of healing from that initial trauma.

263

We might experience trauma as an emotional shift or cognitive overload in the present. Typically, any strong emotion that doesn't match the current situation is associated with a past experience or scar that reminds us of the current situation. So, a simple tool that I use is to turn to curiosity as quickly as possible whenever I or someone I encounter undergoes a drastic shift in emotions due to a triggering situation. The sooner we can start supporting ourselves or another person in the present, the sooner we may begin to seek to repair the initial trauma at the root of the reaction.

The way to heal and have a more measured or appropriately matching reaction to a similar situation in the future is to access and relive the original trauma from a more resourced place. If we can find the tools to survive or heal that original trauma—be it the strength, size, and agency to protect ourselves physically or perhaps the confidence, awareness, and language to protect our emotional safety—we can lay down new neural pathways for when our nervous system encounters similar situations in the future.

When it comes to facilitating, we may hear a response that triggers a reaction in us. Perhaps an insensitive word is used, or a past relatable and still painful trauma is shared by another person. Once we are triggered, our minds might shift into a place of introspection, projection, and judgment. These reactions alert and activate our ego in order to remain safe. We become personally attached to the situation and outcome, because our ego believes we are in danger. In a triggered state, we are a bit sped up and can't tell the difference between reality and an abnormal emotional reaction. However, when we access this interaction slowly and from a detached place, our cognitive mind remembers and reassures our nervous system that the words it is reacting to don't match the emotional response they are causing. At the very least, we know that if physical harm is not imminent, the emotional charge the words cause in you is likely temporary. You have the tools to acknowledge, label, accept, remedy, or move through the temporary lapse in psychological safety.

I always recommend establishing ground rules to create safety whenever facilitating a conversation that has the potential to be triggering. This may be as simple as informing friends and family of what they are getting into ahead of time, or as formal as sharing a walk-through of rules that protect safety. Some ground rules that I like to share include the following:

Vault: What's said here, stays here. What's learned here, leaves here.

Your experience: Share from the heart and not the head, and use "I" statements to ground in your own experience.

Safe space: Honor the wisdom of others by giving uninterrupted space to share.

Notes: Listen to urges to interrupt and take note of movements of elevated emotion.

Share the air: Help others feel heard and be mindful of length and frequency of shares.

No questions asked: If you need to pause to take space, do so—no questions asked.

265

Should a situation arise when a person is experiencing a triggering event, you might observe them exhibiting a loss of words or clarity (flight or freeze), anger or agitation (fight), or elevated emotion or mismatched reactions (flight or fawn). The way to support in these instances is to remain grounded yourself, or to temporarily shift your own emotions to mirror theirs before returning to a more grounded place. Your actions will ensure that the person is affirmed in their emotional state and safe to access and regulate their emotions with your help. You should immediately remind the other person that they are safe, you are there to support,

"You can connect to the other person by matching their breathing cadence."

and that they can always take a break with no questions asked. You can connect to the other person by matching their breathing cadence and using your own breathing to model slowing down. You may invite them to share their physical and emotional experience instead of or ahead of sharing more details about their reaction or response. You can affirm them throughout, and after, for taking the risk to experience and share what is happening for them. Let them know that what they are feeling and experiencing is normal and totally OK. Go slow and trust yourself and them to experience the miracle of healing.

It may seem scary and even a bit unsafe to support a person through a triggering experience. However, the process of encountering an emotionally triggering experience and navigating through it to a place of safety helps all participants involved strengthen their resilience. Even simply observing the wave of emotions from another person helps you have greater clarity should you encounter a similar situation in the future in your own life.

When in groups, if someone or several people appear to be triggered, some questions you might ask yourself or the group include the following:

Is the triggering emotion a signal of something personal that will take you out of observation and into judgment or ego? Is the group affected or is it just me?

Am I triggered or projecting? Triggered means a sensitive memory has been engaged and is forcing the ego to speak up. Projecting means you've begun to merge your own story and needs with that of the person you are supporting. You are giving the advice and support you would want, rather than remaining present to the reactions and needs of the person or group.

Does anyone need to take space for themselves to feel safe before we move forward?

These questions help you attune to yourself and resource yourself. As a facilitator, you aren't as effective if you are feeling the need to tend to your ego. It's likely a sign that you feel unsafe and need to take care of yourself first. Do the internal work to scan, label, and choose to let go or address what you are feeling. Once you have gone through this progression, typically you will find it easier to attune to the group. Also, you might find that your own share might echo sentiments that others in the group are experiencing, allowing others the room to relax, open, and connect. Either way, you are modeling to the group what assertive vulnerability looks like.

When encountering a triggering situation, you might consider these questions: "Is the triggering emotion a signal of something that has been said that will severely damage the safety of the space that has been created? Has the safety of the container been damaged or is this an example of healthy friction?" If this is the case, a more intentional intervention might be required to repair and reset safety. You might quickly contemplate these questions: "Can I continue to moderate and let the situation unfold? Or do I need to slow the situation down and create the opportunity for a reset and to repair the container?" For a facilitator, it's important to allow for discomfort and disharmony. Some of the most impactful learning comes through conflict. As individuals, we have more capacity for dysregulation and conflict resolution than we're given credit for. However, facilitators must use their own comfort level and discretion in choosing to call a time-out, separate triggered parties, and allow space for re-regulation of the individual and the group.

Although these situations will be among the most

challenging on your journey into empathy, remember that no one dies from an emotionally triggering situation. You may be worried that you might cause irreparable damage. You won't. You need only navigate the situation at hand and learn crucial lessons for the future. To de-escalate or seek help in an elevated situation, think through the following steps:

Slow down or stop: Intervene in the situation. Stop the flow of conversation and energy and acknowledge what you are observing. If the container has been damaged, say that. Share that there will be time to unpack what happened and repair.

Breathe: You may need to regulate your breathing to stay calm while using that grounded space to prompt controlled breathing for the elevated individual and possibly the group. Three deep breaths in and three slow exhales is scientifically proven to reduce fear and anger.

Trust: Remind yourself of your intent rather than fixating on the challenge at hand. The reason you are in the role of facilitator remains, regardless of the outcome of this specific facilitation. Humans and groups are resilient. We can handle more emotional expression than we are given credit for.

Separate and get help: Always remind the people involved that it is OK to separate, go off screen or leave the room, and take time for their own self-care and recovery. For someone who appears distressed, a gentle inquiry in private or afterward can go a long way to helping them feel supported. Finally, as we aren't therapists, it's important to acknowledge that fact up front and afterward. Be prepared with contacts and resources to offer support if additional professional guidance will be useful.

The role of empathetic leader has many benefits, but typically they come paired with the responsibility of engaging with the mental well-being of those you are supporting. Although you can't predict all scenarios, you can think through your plan of action should you encounter a difficult triggering situation.

DAY 28

Exercise

On Day 28, I'd like to share some journaling prompts and advice to prepare you for difficult and potentially triggering conversations.

What will you do if the conversation creates a powerful or uncomfortable response for you?

Breathe and slow down.

Consider if the trigger is yours or something felt by the majority of the group. Has it expanded the emotional territory or damaged the safety of the group?

Choose to intervene or to let the situation unfold.

How can you use vulnerable bravery to catch your breath and recenter your thoughts?

Create an intervention and share your own experience by saying, "Excuse me, I need to slow down and share something in order to remain present."

Start by sharing what you feel in your body and naming the moment that caused it. Label the sensations using the five core emotions. Allow the group space to integrate their own reactions.

How can you use humor appropriately to respond to a triggering situation?

Use humor sparingly as a tool to create safety or defuse a tense situation rather than as a distraction from challenging discussions.

Simple phrases like "Is it me, or did things just get really intense?" might bring out the shared desire to return to harmony with a moment of laughter.

Sharing a story from your past in which a tense situation occurred and a deeper connection followed the conflict might allow the group to externalize the process of recovery, providing a map of how to repair the harm done.

How can you acknowledge your own emotions while also modeling growth?

Recap what happened for you in real time.

Acknowledge that a triggering moment breached your or others' safety in the group.

Recap the process of slowing down and defaulting to vulnerability, showing that it was safe to experience and express the emotions that arose.

Celebrate how the group co-moderated, co-regulated, and navigated from one point to another.

Explore what you have observed in yourself. Your intentional awareness expands your emotional growth and supplies you with a road map that others can also use to grow from challenging or triggering situations.

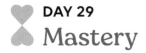

Mastery

What does growth look like for you over the next twelve months?

Progress and growth look different for everyone. For some, it's a period when you give yourself permission to do less. For others, there may be a fear or block or even lack of clarity standing in the way of healing, desires, and dreams. Whatever that area of exploration may be, you've just strengthened your emotional capacity to achieve it. Day 29, Mastery, is both about reflecting on how far we've come in our empathy journey and about offering encouragement for continued progress. Your potential for self-empathy, your understanding of others, and the impact you will have on the world around you are infinite. Our goal is to set you up with new rituals for creating emotional elasticity and expansiveness.

Mastery is depth of knowledge in a skill or subject area. Those who achieve the level of mastery push well beyond the typical level of comprehension of the subject. They reach the point where pursuit of knowledge becomes difficult and laborious, and they keep going. They unlock levels of understanding that have been reached by very few. When we started this journey on Day 1, many of you didn't know what to expect or how you might respond to the teaching, exercises, and prompts. Now you have only two days left. This book and the journey we've taken together is an analogy for the work of returning to individual and collective emotional awareness. By reaching this point, you've already proven your capacity to feel, experience, learn, and grow.

For me, mastery happens when I start to crave growth rather than fear it. It's when we become addicted to growth—finding the imperfections, loving them, and turning them into superpowers—that we discover happiness in change and share that passion with others. For me, this shift happened in the summer of 2021 when I felt I was nearing a different kind of emotional rock bottom: burnout. I was several months into an entrepreneur in residency, leading a steady ongoing consumer workshop every Sunday, running the cards business, and dreaming up new ways to spread empathy through content and partnerships. We were getting frequent calls to lead empathy workshops for various organizations. I reached a place where I could not keep my thoughts together. Interactions with potential workshop clients were bringing about fear and anxiety. My body was frequently tense. I was becoming short-fused with my team and even Caroline. Something needed to change.

I felt that the workshops were taking a toll on me physically and emotionally. I also began to realize that by being deeply embedded with a few organizations, I was beginning to take on their fears and anxieties. I couldn't compartmentalize. I sought out a few facilitation

trainings with the explicit goal of understanding myself better. I was learning to process and let go, to be a better facilitator, but also to take care of myself in the process.

Part of the burnout was caused by my preparation and rituals after the workshops. I didn't allow myself space before workshops to get grounded or after workshops to release. I was scheduling too many workshops in the same day or week. I had to learn how much rest I needed, and at what frequency I could do facilitation and still have enough. Ultimately, I decided to drastically reduce the number of workshops I accepted, which was difficult to do because they paid well and provided a level of security that my team and I had become used to.

To prioritize my long-term well-being, I decided to take a risk. I would develop my ideas and intellectual property. This meant forgoing guaranteed wages now for the internal

"The writing of this book became my latest pursuit in the mastery of empathy."

benefit of realizing my ideas, as well as the belief in a future material payoff. That was a scary and shame-inducing choice to make. I was afraid of failure and of the anticipated reactions of my family, friends, and peers. I took those risks, small and big, and I survived. This process proved to me again that I have the tools to work through scary and challenging emotions.

I redirected the extra energy into outlining this book, *The Power of Empathy*. I realized that I enjoyed spreading the tools of empathy—but my physical, emotional, and time limitations wouldn't allow me to be in all the spaces I wanted to be in. I had to accept my limitations as an introvert and as a human being. I knew the Five Phases of Empathy and our empathy workshop had a valuable role to play in society, and delivering it in a book format would provide me the opportunity to share it with far more people than I'd be able to reach

in person. Through the process of conceiving and writing the book, I found the opportunity to explore my edges and areas of growth around empathy. The writing of this book became my latest pursuit in the mastery of empathy. It took me two months to write the proposal. I worked with book agents, and less than six months later, I received three offers with advances. In the same year that I signed that book deal, I bought my first home, had my first child, and began fundraising for acceleration partners for the Curiosity Lab movement to spread empathy. Before the close of 2022, we received an investment from Pharrell Williams' Black Ambition Prize competition. You might say that mastery of my emotions is moving my ambition and my purpose forward at a breakneck pace. But it no longer feels that way to me, as I'm able to remain grounded and in the present moment in spite of the speed at which things are moving.

273

DAY 29

Exercise

On Day 29, I invite you to identify sources of pride in your journey over the past month. Using the following journaling prompts, find moments of gratitude and explore areas of desired stretching and growth. Our work goes as far as possible before the reset.

How have you used your newly acquired empathy skills?

What discoveries have you made about yourself?

Were there any aha! moments?

As you reflect on this personal inventory of growth, what do you feel excited to do next now that you have the tools to make positive emotional and social changes through the power of empathy? Are there areas where you'd like to continue to improve? What topics might you like to explore in more depth?

DAY 30

Zero Mindset

What would starting over look like to you? Easier, harder? Full of joy? Full of challenges? A mixture of it all?

When we were born, we were empty of ideas, experiences, projections, and trauma— perhaps the purest state of happiness. Soon after, the world around us began to form who we are. *The Power of Empathy* is an invitation to start from the beginning, bringing conscious acknowledgment of our pasts into how we engage with our present and future. On our last day, Day 30, Zero Mindset, we'll reflect on our growth since Day 1, and I will leave you with a set of powerful questions that you can revisit in your reflection and journaling practice. These questions will help you ground in gratitude, grow, and contribute to the world from a place of self-empathy, resilience, consistency, humility, and love.

In the beginning of this journey, I asked what empathy meant to you. I personally revisit this

question often with an expectation that I might learn something totally new, and often I do. It's not that the old definitions of empathy fade away; it's that the layers around and inside of the term expand. We as individuals and as groups work that way. We are constantly growing and learning about ourselves and changing everything and everyone we touch in that process, too. The realization of how we change and respond to change didn't crystallize for me until 2019, when I experienced so much loss all at once.

The loss of my two brothers in addition to the dysfunctional relationships and coping mechanisms that supported me back then taught me that to navigate change, loss, and suffering, I needed more empathy and understanding for myself. The intense suffering inside and around me at the time helped me navigate toward empathy as a tool for survival, healing, rebirth, and renewal.

I had to learn the true meaning of the phrase "this too shall pass." Books and thought leadership on grief say you need to acknowledge, feel, and process to heal and eventually move forward through loss. Years later, there are still times where I go through the cycle of acknowledging, feeling, and processing those losses. The intensity of the pain I felt back then, the anger and shame, has drastically lessened. The sadness has not passed. Reminders throughout life, like knowing my children will never meet Chris and Darren, still bring me back to the initial moment of loss.

"This too shall pass" reminds of the good moments as well as the difficult. Thoughts of my brothers also bring me back to the moments that forged our bonds. The moments of joy that I experienced in the past with family, friends, and even lovers that I've lost remind me that there were phenomenal times that colored and created the life that I'm leading. The moments that nourish

me help me move to a place of gratitude for the time that I spent with my loved ones.

By returning to zero, I mean trying to find the earliest experiences we remember that shaped who we are and how we feel. If I go back as far as I can, starting from a point of zero, I can see that the reason losing loved ones hurt so bad was because of the experiences of joy that we had together in this physical world. Returning to zero helps strengthen the resources of reflection, acceptance, gratitude, and letting go to help us carry on.

As we experience change, and specifically loss, the physical presence of a person changes. None of us can avoid that. The emotional quality of a relationship, in life and in the afterlife, also changes. Our memories, in some ways, also change when we subconsciously or consciously focus our lens on one aspect or another. When we anticipate the changes that will occur around us, we strengthen the muscles needed to heal from the tough parts by turning to gratitude for the parts we cherish.

The cycle of life and death, for me, is a unifying opportunity for collective empathy. We can all relate to these pivotal moments and how they affect and change us on an emotional level. We are changed by these moments, and we can also learn through observing them.

For me, birthdays are moments when individuals change and when groups come together in rituals of celebration and acknowledgment. For me, birthdays are hard, because they weren't greatly celebrated in my family. When I attuned to the shame I had for not knowing how to celebrate birthdays with elevated joy, I began to feel compassion for the likely lack of celebratory joy in my parents' lives. This was and still is a painful cycle of acknowledgment to work through, but it reminds me that I have a choice to create a

different experience for myself in the present and for my children in their future. It may take time to heal the wounds that extend further generationally than we can see, but returning to zero gives us the chance to create a different experience for our families and for those who can relate to this mission. I am and we are at zero right now.

From birthdays, to weddings, to the change of the season, to the turn of the new year, we encounter moments when we individually and collectively acknowledge cycles of change. Use them as a reminder to return to zero. You now have the ability to bring awareness, and willingness to embrace change, into your holistic knowledge of people and situations. Our pasts will always remain, but how we choose to engage with them can start at zero.

We are programmed to reset, yet few of us take the option. We sleep, we wake, we reset. We breath in, we breath out, we

277

reset. *The Power of Empathy* teaches us that every opportunity to reset is an opportunity for curiosity and wisdom. A chance to take a second look with fresh eyes and learn what we don't already know.

It brings me joy to think of this concept through an analogy to a goldfish and to a tree. A goldfish, they say, is one of the happiest creatures on planet Earth. They don't live incredibly long, but they are always happy because their memories don't last very long. Every ten seconds feels completely new; they can never get bored. A tree, however, can live for hundreds or thousands of years. If you look at a cut of a tree branch or its bark through a microscope you can see that it stores memories of every year that it has lived. Too many memories even to be concerned with any one bad year or moment. The tree remembers and adapts to survive. The tree even communicates with the rest of the plant world underground through

its roots, giving and receiving support as it is able.

We can learn to be like the goldfish, forgetting and returning to zero. We have that power in us. We can also, like trees, benefit from an internal wisdom and pass that wisdom along organically through the ways that we live, and the ways we adapt and survive.

Day 30, Zero Mindset, is an invitation to be like both the goldfish and the tree. We can choose to return to joy by healing and moving on from the past and returning to what is new, present, and possible. We can find happiness, connection, and longevity by tending to our needs for survival in the present and by sharing knowledge and tools for healing and survival over the course of our lives on this earth.

The Power of Empathy teaches us that how we engage with our friends, romantic partners, job, hobbies, and passions is as much about the values we absorbed from our past as it is about how we recognize and process our emotions. Each interaction we have, the nourishing ones as well as the challenging ones, is an opportunity to return to zero. Ask yourself, "What happened then and what can I learn to help improve my life today?" From there, you can discover what safety, trust, and healthy relationships look like for you. Past, present, and future experiences expand our knowledge and provide greater ease in using empathy in our day-to-day lives.

It is inevitable that we will encounter issues with health in our families and friend groups, as well as in ourselves. When dealing with our families and friends through health issues, our lack of control can be the most debilitating part. It is a difficult experience for all who are involved when supporting a family member through a lifelong disability or a terminal illness, yet it is in our nature to rise to the challenge and figure it out. The resilience all around us is remarkable. Use these adversities as another signal to return to zero. Ask yourself, "How can I provide better support to myself and all involved today, tomorrow, and the next day?"

It can be even harder perhaps to support an individual who is working through addiction or addiction- or diet-related illnesses. These scenarios require that we find the compassion to look past that individual's hand in their fate to offer them compassion. It might be easier and perhaps even justified to move to judgment, but the more helpful and proactive approach would be to emulate the goldfish here. Ask yourself, "How can I support right now?" But also be like the tree. Ask, "How can I use wisdom to honor my boundaries and resources?"

We can have these same challenges when dealing with our own ups and downs. Even for the healthiest among us, there will come a day when our bodies will begin to change and eventually fail us. Will our hearts and minds be ready for that day and respond with love and compassion, rather than fear, shame, anger, and sadness?

To support ourselves through healing and growth, we have to first believe that we have the power to do so. To support others in partnership, friendship, and love over the long haul, we can begin to attune to their needs around safety, healing, and growth. We become aware of and protective of the "third body." We become

proactive players in protecting the emotional safety of our groups, making sure all voices are heard. But to do so, we first must be able to approach others from a place of love.

A vibration of love and a vibration of fear cannot exist simultaneously. Healthy ideas and connections are created when you are in a place to receive and give love. When we are closed off, fearful of what might happen, we project that through our body language, the subtleties of our words, and our actions. We cannot attract love when we are in this state. We have control over where we land in this space by strengthening our ability to return to zero.

When times are good, we recharge, we expand, and we recreate. When times are challenging, we slow down, we learn from the past, and we have compassion for the rough parts. Our long-term view and wisdom allow us to prepare to show up the way we want

> ## "The convenient part is that the classroom for learning is your life."

to—grounded, confident, intentional, and effective.

Over the last thirty days, we've honed our empathy abilities for the more challenging moments ahead. I've provided an introduction to concepts in psychology, neuroscience, conflict resolution, trust building, group therapy, and leadership development that can be applied in our practical lives to heal ourselves, sharpen our focus, expand our capacity for compassion, and lead us toward good deeds and living well. The work of mastery sits with you. You master empathy as a skill, just as you would train for a sport or a job. With practice it becomes easier and you inevitably get better. The convenient part is that the classroom for learning is your life—your past, your present, and your future. And lessons are found in our interactions, our community structures, our governments, our geopolitics, and our relationship to the galaxy at large.

I wrote this book to provide accessible and relatable support and training as a gift to the world. It can be daunting, this gift of empathy that many of us have. It leads us to caring, and to extending ourselves because of that care. It leads us to professions that we love, that perhaps do not love us back. It leads us at times to giving more than we receive in return. It leads us to showing love and support in places that might be insatiable. In spite of the dangers, we show our empathy because it makes us feel good. *The Power of Empathy* is permission to do whatever that is for you, in a way that supports your well-being and happiness, for as long as you possibly can.

The Power of Empathy is a reminder that by embracing the well-being and happiness of the collective, we receive immediate emotional benefits while unlocking greater support, resources, and love for ourselves in the long run.

As we close our journey together, Day 30, Zero Mindset, reminds us that we are never trapped; we can always start over. Many of us are forced to endure much more suffering than we deserve. But perhaps the sad truth is that far more of us self-inflict suffering and hinder our own freedom and well-being.

By returning to our simplest truths—what we feel and what we value—we find there is great abundance afforded us.

The power of empathy is recognizing the universality of life, death, and the suffering we experience in between. It's about opening ourselves to the experiences of vulnerability and compassion, which, while difficult at times, deepens our understanding of the precious gift (not burden) that is life. It helps us develop the knowledge and strength to provide support to others, as well as the wisdom to guide our lives from a place of gratitude for our daily gifts.

DAY 30

Exercise

On Day 30, we will explore some powerful questions that help us reflect on our growth since Day 1 and amplify our gratitude for our resilience, consistency, and humility. These questions can also guide you in supporting someone who needs help with grounding in gratitude and self-compassion.

Was waking up this morning a promise or a blessing?

Do you feel safe at this moment? If not, what must you do right now to create safety for yourself?

Do you feel like you are living in your integrity? If not, what's the first thing your values and purpose tell you to do?

What is guaranteed to bring you happiness?

What makes you unique?

A Shared Pursuit of Happiness

Thank you for coming on this journey with me. We conclude here by exploring our commonalities on a practical, biological, intellectual, and emotional level. We aspire to similar things, and by advocating for one another's happiness and well-being, we directly invest in our own. I'll close here with a challenge that encourages turning some of the skills you've learned across these past thirty days into a ritual:

Establish a regular mindfulness routine.

Reevaluate your values when needed.

Audit your values alignment.

Make fear one of your best friends.

Check your bias and judgment.

Be intentional about your contribution.

Dream and manifest.

Share your gifts.

Return to zero.

Acknowledgments

To those who have supported my dream with their emotions, sense of purpose, energy, and consistency: thank you. I would not have been inspired to write this book if it weren't for the contributions, big and small, direct and indirect, of a vanguard of humans who believe in the power of empathy.

Caroline, thank you for your belief in our partnerships in love, business, parenthood, and healing. You have been the safety net that has allowed me to climb higher each day without fear of falling. You have opened your heart and allowed me to learn how to open mine. You are the first domino, the one thing. Receiving your love and attention changed my life and gave me the greatest gift of all, Lady Naya. Her life will be a testament to our ongoing work to expand our compassion, vulnerability, trust, and growth.

My nuclear family, Barbara and Ralton Tennant, and eldest brother, Ralton Tennant Jr., have all overcome a bevy of emotions differently, exhibiting vision, commitment through challenge, consistency, grit, and resilience. They dreamt, survived, provided, and modeled responsibility. They still do.

Thank you to my nieces and nephews who inspire me with their courage, depth, complexity, and ambition.

The support I receive from a spiritual place must be acknowledged: my brothers, Chris and Darren and Kevin Wilkinsen; the ancestors who wish abundance for me; your ancestors, with their eternal wisdom and perspective, wishing safety and happiness for us all.

Thanks to my men's group—Tom, Akash, Daniel, Avi, Alex, Brian, Lionel, Andy, Adam—for the cocreation of the most nurturing primary partnership I've ever experienced. Your strength and gentleness laid the pathway for my personal transformation.

Our teammates and collaborators at Curiosity Lab: Your energy contributions have amplified our work spreading tools for empathy. You've allowed me to channel my energy toward an altruistic vision for happiness and contribution to the world. Morgan, Claudia, Sonali, Rebecca, Kwamz, Megan, Greg, Jace, Raheem, Candice, Synead, Earl, Chris, thank you.

Todd and Jermaine, thank you for your brotherhood in bringing this book to life.

Natalie and the team at Chronicle, thank you for believing in this project and the impact we can manifest together.

I share my gratitude for support from esteemed communities, including BMe Community, Starts With Us, Maynard Institute, and Black Ambition. Thank you, Trabian, Tom, Daniel, Mark, Felicia, and Pharrell.

And to my readers who have seen something in themselves and in the world around them that they are willing to fight for, thank you, and welcome to the movement to spread empathy.

References

Introduction

Reinert, Maddy, Theresa Nguyen, and Danielle Fritze. "The State of Mental Health in America 2021, 2020." https://mhanational.org/sites/default/files/2021%20State%20of%20Mental%20Health%20in%20America_0.pdf.

Health Resources and Services Administration/National Center for Health Workforce Analysis; Substance Abuse and Mental Health Services Administration/Office of Policy, Planning, and Innovation. 2015. "National Projections of Supply and Demand for Behavioral Health Practitioners: 2013–2025." https://bhw.hrsa.gov/sites/default/files/bureau-health-workforce/data-research/behavioral-health-2013-2025.pdf.

Health Resources and Services Administration, "Health Workforce Shortage Areas," HRSA Data Warehouse, last accessed December 28, 2022. https://data.hrsa.gov/topics/health-workforce/shortage-areas.

PHASE ONE
Day 1

"Empathy." *Oxford Learner's Dictionaries.* Last accessed October 17, 2022. https://www.oxfordlearnersdictionaries.com/definition/english/empathy.

Psychology Today staff. "Empathy." *Psychology Today.* Last accessed November 14, 2022. https://www.psychologytoday.com/us/basics/empathy.

PuddleDancer Press. "Marshall Rosenberg's NVC Quotes." Nonviolent Communication Books & Resources. Last accessed November 14, 2022. https://www.nonviolentcommunication.com/resources/mbr-quotes.

Day 2

Bureau of Labor Statistics, US Department of Labor. "American Time Use Survey—2021 Results." June 23, 2022. https://www.bls.gov/news.release/pdf/atus.pdf.

Todorov, Georgi. "Important Burnout Stats, Trends and Facts 2022." Last updated October 17, 2022. https://thrivemyway.com/burnout-stats.

Reinert, Maddy, Theresa Nguyen, and Danielle Fritze. "The State of Mental Health in America 2021, 2020." https://mhanational.org/sites/default/files/2021%20State%20of%20Mental%20Health%20in%20America_0.pdf.

Patel, Jainish, and Prittesh Patel. "Consequences of Repression of Emotion: Physical Health, Mental Health and General Well Being." *International Journal of Psychotherapy Practice and Research* 1, no. 3 (February 15, 2019): 16–21. https://openaccesspub.org/ijpr/article/999.

The Dalai Lama and Desmond Tutu. *The Book of Joy: Lasting Happiness in a Changing World.* New York: Avery Publishing, 2016.

Day 3

Ott, Crystal. "What Is Emotional Intelligence?" Ohio 4-H Youth Development. Ohio State University Extension. https://ohio4h.org /sites/ohio4h/files/imce/Emotional%20 Intelligence%20Background.pdf.

"Empathy—An Overview." *ScienceDirect.* Last accessed November 9, 2022.

Day 5

University of California Santa Barbara Health & Wellness. "Happiness Challenge: Mindfulness." Last accessed November 9, 2022. https:// wellness.ucsb.edu/challenges/happiness -challenge/ucsb-happiness-challenge /happiness-challenge-mindfulness.

PHASE TWO

Marchant, Jerem. "Projection." *Emotional Intelligence at Work.* 2007. http://www .emotionalintelligenceatwork.com/resources /projection.

Psychology Today staff. "Projection." *Psychology Today.* Last accessed November 9, 2022. https://www.psychologytoday.com/us /basics/projection.

Greene, Robert. *The Laws of Human Nature.* New York: Viking Press, 2018.

Day 10

World Health Organization staff. WHO Coronavirus (Covid-19) Dashboard. Last accessed November 9, 2022. https://covid19 .who.int/.

Finkbeiner, Ann. "The Biology of Grief." *New York Times.* April 22, 2021. https://www.nytimes .com/2021/04/22/well/what-happens-in-the -body-during-grief.html.

PHASE THREE

Day 12

Kämmerer, Annette. "The Scientific Underpinnings and Impacts of Shame." *Scientific American.* 2020, 2021. https://www .scientificamerican.com/article/the-scientific -underpinnings-and-impacts-of-shame.

Day 13

"Ego," Encyclopedia Britannica. December 15, 2021. https://www.britannica.com/topic/ego -philosophy-and-psychology.

PHASE FIVE

Day 21

Scanlan, Stephen J., J. Craig Jenkins, and Lindsey Peterson. "The Scarcity Fallacy." *Contexts* 9, no. 3 (February 1, 2010): 34–39. https://journals.sagepub.com/doi/pdf/10.1525 /ctx.2010.9.1.34.

Day 22

Lev-Tov, Devorah. "How an Empathy Expert Spends His Sundays." *New York Times.* October 16, 2020. https://www.nytimes.com/2020/10/16 /nyregion/actually-curious-michael-tennant .html.

Day 24

McWilliams, Lizzie. "New EY Consulting Survey Confirms 90% of US Workers Believe Empathetic Leadership Leads to Higher Job Satisfaction and 79% Agree It Decreases Employee Turnover." Ernst & Young (press release). October 14, 2021. https://www.ey.com/en_us /news/2021/09/ey-empathy-in-business-survey.

Day 25

Craven, Sister Jan. "Definition of a Miracle." Sisters of Providence of Saint Mary-of-the-Woods. 2015. https://spsmw.org/2015/08/18 /definition-of-a-miracle/.

Day 26

Centers for Disease Control and Prevention, Kaiser Permanente. "The ACE Study Survey Data." (Unpublished data.) Atlanta, GA: U.S. Department of Health and Human Services, Centers for Disease Control and Prevention. 2016. https://www.cdc.gov/violenceprevention /aces/about.html.

Herman, Judith L. "Recovery from Psychological Trauma." *Psychiatry and Clinical Neurosciences* 52 (January 4, 2002): S98–S103. https://doi .org/10.1046/j.1440-1819.1998.0520s5S145.x.

MORE RESOURCES

Goleman, Daniel, and Paul Ekman. Wired to Connect: Dialogues on Social Intelligence series. (Key Step Media)

Healthline. "Let It Out: Dealing with Repressed Emotions." Last updated March 31, 2020. https://www.healthline.com/health/repressed -emotions.

Thompson, Nicholas. "Chapter 15: Empathy." In *Neuroimaging Personality, Social Cognition, and Character*. Edited by John R. Absher and Jasmin Cloutier. London: Academic Press, 2016. 289–303. https://doi.org/10.1016/B978-0-12 -800935-2.00015-4.